# A SOLICITOR'S GUIDE TO COMPLAINTS AVOIDANCE AND HANDLING

## DEDICATION

I would like to gratefully acknowledge the support and assistance afforded me in the preparation of this book by my colleagues Peter Johnson, Stuart Waterworth for his help in the section dealing with Probate issues and Geoff Negus for his unstinting encouragement throughout.

# A SOLICITOR'S GUIDE TO COMPLAINTS AVOIDANCE AND HANDLING

**Michael Frith,**
LlB, Solicitor

xpl

NOTE:

In this book there are many references to the current arm of the Law Society involved in the regulation of the profession, the Consumer Complaints Service (CCS). Where reference is to the OSS (the predecessor of the CCS) it is because the particular example being referred to relates to that body.

© Michael Frith 2004

Published by
XPL Publishing
31–33 Stonehills House
Welwyn Garden City
Hertfordshire
AL8 6PU

ISBN 1 85811 328 8

Typeset by Saxon Graphics Ltd, Derby
Printed and bound in the UK by Lightning Source International

# CONTENTS

*solicitor – think about the response – the lay-out of letters – using appropriate sentences and words – having letters checked – avoiding adverbs – DON'T BLAME THE CLIENT – accounting errors – KEEP AN OPEN MIND – conceding justified complaints – looking behind the complaint – explaining unjustified complaints – the closed mind syndrome*

# PREFACE

Never before, in the legal profession, have the issues of client care and client complaints assumed such a high profile as they do at present. It is, therefore, surprising that, at a time when the subject is receiving constant publicity and the profession are being continually urged to become ever more client-focussed, there is no text on those subjects to which a solicitor can turn for guidance.

This publication seeks to remedy the defect. Throughout the masculine implies the feminine.

The book follows on from a series of lectures presented by the author countrywide over the last 3½ years, to great acclaim, and develops, and expands upon, the content of those lectures. In doing so, the author has drawn on his considerable experience, both as a solicitor in typical High Street practice (28 years), his work as a Senior Complaints handler dealing with service complaints made against solicitors (five years) and advising members of the profession at first hand about problems they have come up against in dealing with service complaints (five years). He has also served as Honorary Secretary of his local Law Society, for ten years, and then as President.

# PART ONE:
## AVOIDING COMPLAINTS

# CHAPTER ONE
# THE CHARACTERISTICS
# OF A COMPLAINT

It is a specific and important part of Client Care that complaints are handled properly when they arise. Hopefully, any firm that embraces a proper Client Care policy, will find the scope for complaints to arise will be substantially reduced. However, there will still be circumstances that will give rise to complaints. It is essential that practitioners are made aware of the factors and circumstances that contribute to complaints arising in order that they can, if at all possible, be avoided.

The first priority is to gain an appreciation of what are the main factors that cause complaints. Experience teaches that, as a rule, there are not very many characteristics that cause a client to complain, but those that there are crop up time and time again and are common across all disciplines – no matter what kind of work it is that the practitioner does.

In March 2003, The Law Society published what it called its Client Charter. Primarily intended for the general public, it listed eleven things that a solicitor would do when acting for a client. The failure to do seven of these form the five main heads of complaint – and that isn't double-dutch! It's just that the Law Society chose to split two of the causes of complaint into two separate parts.

Before we consider the main causes of complaint, it would be appropriate to offer a few words on preliminary issues that seem to cause problems across the profession where complaints are concerned and are matters about which practitioners need to be clear at the outset.

The first is that what follows in this book is all about the genuine complainant. There is a great temptation to believe that virtually every complainant has an ulterior motive – usually to avoid paying the bill. The great problem with that is, that not only is it untrue, but it also leads the solicitor to adopt a dismissive, defensive or confrontational, approach to the complaint. This does nothing to resolve the issue at hand, particularly when the complaint is a genuine concern the client has, and simply makes matters worse. The client resents the response and determines to take matters further. He digs his heels in and so, what could, and should, perhaps, have been a relatively simple matter to resolve, now assumes nightmarish proportions which is going to consume literally hours of time – and it still won't be satisfactorily resolved for either solicitor and client when it has run its course.

Time and again Caseworkers at the CCS despair when they come across a complaint that should never have been allowed to get off the ground, but, because of the solicitor's attitude, has arrived at the CCS, and, because the complaint is justified anyway, is now going to cost the practitioner dear in terms of costs, compensation and wasted fee-earning time.

There is a great temptation to think that one has a serial, persistent or professional complainant when one gets one of those complaints that arrive tied in brown paper and lands on the desk with a thump. One starts to read it with sinking heart because it appears to be a lot of repetitive rubbish.

Don't be misled. Even those complaints usually have a root cause that is a genuine concern that the client has – and he has probably bottled up inside him for some time. It is that which has led to the size of the complaint. While the grievance has been festering away, it has grown, incorporating all manner of niggles that would never normally have seen the light of day as a complaint, but as it has grown, so the client has convinced himself that even those niggles are fully justified complaints. And there is one of the causes of complaint that will be dealt with later which is primarily responsible for that kind of monster complaint.

One consolation is that, no matter what is the general opinion, there aren't many people like that! If you have one, you usually know it before the complaint arrives because of the client's behaviour.

If you have a client who seeks to query and complain about everything and anything, then the chances are that you have got one and the only thing that can be done is to get rid of them as soon as possible. The perfect excuse exists. If ever there was any proper solicitor/client relationship, there isn't now! Trust – that vital constituent element in any solicitor/client relationship – has gone out of the window. The down-side is that the complaints still have to be dealt with at face value.

It is entirely possible, however, that if you genuinely have got a serial complainer on your hands they are known to the CCS, who will not entertain their complaint. Some amazing examples exist. Like the lady who over the course of several months complained about fifty-four different firms of solicitors in Birmingham. Or the lady in Nottingham who was sending in complaints at the rate of a minimum of two per week, and sometimes two per day!

The next two points cause confusion in the profession. The first is that you are only supposed to be dealing with service complaints from your clients – and, with one exception, no-one else, unless you have the specific written authority from your client to do so. The exception arises in Probate complaints and will be dealt with later in the Chapter dealing with Probate complaints.

However, no matter how close the relationship is between your client and the would-be complainant, unless you have your client's authority, you cannot deal with it. Instead a letter should be written to the would-be complainant, explaining that you cannot deal with the issues that they seek to raise because they are not the client and if you were to do so, you would be in breach of your duty of confidentiality to your client.

Very often the CCS comes across cases where close relatives, who often have not been kept fully appraised of all developments by the client, seek to take up perceived issues on behalf of their spouse, or parent or child, whereas, in fact, the actual client is quite happy and has no complaint at all.

The second issue is that solicitors are only supposed to be dealing with complaints about their standards of service under their firm's complaints procedure. They are not supposed to be dealing with complaints about standards of work. Such complaints are in reality negligence allegations and should be dealt with as such. Even the Legal Services Ombusdman, who in the shape of their different personae over the years, has tried to pressure the OSS into dealing under the firm's complaints procedure, with what they call "minor issues of negligence" has to admit that solicitors cannot deal with negligence issues for which they are insured.

So, if a complaint is received that amounts to an accusation that the advice given was wrong, or that a case has been pursued wrongly, or that professional judgement has been exercised wrongly or that a better result could and should have been achieved, explain to the client that, although they may not realise it, they are actually suggesting the solicitor has been negligent. If they want to pursue the issue, they should be taking independent legal advice and the matter will be reported to the firm's insurers.

The only exception to this would occur when any monetary result of the complaint claim, at its very maximum, would fall within the firm's excess under their professional indemnity policy.

It is possible, of course, that a letter of complaint will raise issues of both negligence and service. If this is the case, then differentiate between them; deal with the pure service issues and give the proper advice about the negligence issues.

If it is genuinely impossible to make a distinction between the nature of the issues, then it is better to adopt a safety-first attitude and to treat them as negligence allegations. Don't give the professional indemnity insurers the opportunity to try to avoid the insurance cover by saying you have made admissions that you should not have done.

However, there are issues that can never, ever, be negligence – they are always complaints of inadequate service. These include:- inadequate costs information; failing to keep clients informed about what is going on; failing to reply to client communications; failing to account properly to clients, particularly for interest; failing to give clients their file when they ask for it and there is no claim for a lien available; late delivery of the bill; losing the file and delay that does not amount to breaches of a limitation period.

There are several distinctions between service complaints and negligence claims. These include:-

1.  Negligence involves issues about standards of work – service complaints are about standards of service

2.  Negligence issues involve right and wrong. Service complaints do not. With a service issue, what can be right for one person can be wrong for the next.

3.  Financial concerns relate only to negligence claims. Do not try that well-worn rebuttal to a service complaint – "this complaint is totally unjustified, the client hasn't lost a penny!" That is absolutely irrelevant to a service complaint where the only issues are, 'if this complaint is justified, how much distress, frustration, anxiety etc has it occasioned the client?' And, while on that subject, please never also try the other well-worn, but equally irrelevant response – "we did a damn good job for this client and got them a super result." You may have done, but it doesn't mean that your service standards were up to scratch.

4.  Negligence is a claim against the firm. A service complaint is not – it is merely a client trying to tell you why he is unhappy. You do not have to "defend" service complaints and to do so will only make matters worse.

Now, a word about complaints that come in from clients who have terminated the retainer and taken their file off to another firm to complete the matter and who then lodge a complaint. You are expected to deal with the complaint and to communicate with the now former client in an effort to resolve it – they are not someone else's client for this purpose. The original firm's retainer extends to dealing with complaints that arise from it. It may be a courtesy to let the new firm know what is happening, but this does not have to be done if it is preferred not to, but to do so could obviously avoid complications arising.

Finally, firms are not allowed to charge clients for dealing with their complaints, however unjustified they may be. On 5 February 2004 the Compliance Board of the Law Society published a statement covering this point. Any attempt to do so would be regarded as compounding the effect of any finding of inadequacy of service. Dealing with complaints is a regulatory requirement and not something for which a charge to the client can be made.

## THE CAUSES OF COMPLAINT – A FAILURE TO MANAGE EXPECTATIONS

Answer the following questions – honestly!

1.  How many times have you complained about clients who have unreasonable ideas about what they can expect, both in terms of service or results?

2.  Do you accept any responsibility for those clients having their unreasonable ideas?

3.  How many of your clients have any idea at all about legal processes and timescales, how long you will take to reply to letters and at what times of the day you will be available? If the answer is not "all of them" –

4.  Why that should be, after all, you could tell them?

When the response to a complaint is to protest how unreasonable the client is being, it means that the solicitor is looking at matters entirely from his point of view and completely failing to appreciate the client's viewpoint. The solicitor knows the client is being unreasonable and assumes that the client must know it also.

One of the essentials in successfully avoiding complaints or dealing with them when they arise is to appreciate the client's viewpoint. It is easy to say and sometimes very difficult to achieve, but it is a theme that will be found to recur time and again in this book. Even if attention is not drawn to it every time, the underlying message will be there.

It is essential to remember that most clients will have little or no appreciation of the realities of legal processes and procedures in which they are about to become involved, let alone how your office is organised, or what kind of service they can realistically expect.

The problem then is that clients draw their own conclusions – and don't forget they are encouraged by the media to expect perfection – and when they are not told differently, they regard those conclusions as being justified.

It must also be remembered that each individual client will have his own individual ideas about the standard of service he is going to get. As a result, it is inevitable that at least some part of the client's ideas are going to be different to your intentions about the service you are going to provide.

This means that clients will, almost inevitably have *some* unreasonable ideas about what they can achieve or what can be achieved for them, or, for instance, how long a particular matter is likely to take, what are the chances of success etc.

It is, however, essential not to give the client the wrong idea. Like one solicitor who, in his Client Care letter stated "We are available at any time for instant advice and can arrange home visits where necessary." Did the solicitor really intend to offer a 24 hour service, 7 days a week, 52 weeks a year?

To realise how expectations have to be managed it is important to appreciate what yardsticks clients apply when judging standards of service. They tend to be totally different from the yardsticks against which the profession measures its standards.

For a lawyer, "doing a good job" is judged from a technical viewpoint. Fee-earners' abilities are judged on how well they do the work. A negligence claim is seen as far more destructive than taking too long to reply to a client's correspondence. (In terms of reputation, however, the opposite may be true.)

Most clients, however, haven't the slightest idea whether a job has been done well from the technical viewpoint, or not. They are far more concerned to know that the solicitor is interested in them and their problems – and they certainly want to be kept informed about what is going on.

Even sophisticated commercial clients, whatever their standing, do not possess the solicitors expertise and knowledge – that is what they are buying from the lawyer. Clients take expertise for granted.

Clients continually re-assess service standards. They will continue to instruct you as long as they feel they are getting value for money and are not being taken for granted – and that applies to any client, no matter how friendly your relationship with them. As soon as they feel they are being taken for granted, they are off elsewhere and putting the word around that you are someone to be avoided.

It means that a lawyer's benchmarks tend to be objective, whereas a client's never are – they are always subjective. This distinction has to be constantly borne in mind. When examining a file in response to a complaint, a lawyer is likely to be looking for legal errors. Clients are more concerned about how they have been treated and dealt with as people. Simply looking for legal errors will probably lead the lawyer to overlook the real problem that the client has been trying to raise.

The sting in the tail to all this is that clients judge how good a solicitor is, not by his standard of work, but by whether they are given a feeling of confidence, that they are being looked after and that the solicitor is "on the ball".

No doubt everyone would immediately tell a client at the outset of the retainer if it was apparent that what they were seeking to achieve was unreal. It must be done at the beginning because if a client is allowed to go through a matter fondly imagining he is going to get £50,000 when his claim is, in reality, only worth £5,000, the solicitor has a dissatisfied client on his hands, no matter how good a job he does.

And it's the same with service standards – it is essential to correct any misapprehensions right at the beginning of the retainer before the client has the opportunity to feel he is being let down, ignored or forgotten about because the solicitor is not fulfilling his unreasonable expectations. There is only one chance at this, and it is right at the outset of the retainer – there is no second chance. If you leave it until the complaint is made or it is sensed that the client is becoming "itchy", it is far too late. It doesn't matter what the client is then told, justified though it may be. He will now regard what he is told, not as reasons, but as excuses to justify the solicitor's shortcomings.

It has been known for a complainant to complain of delay because a solicitor had taken 2 weeks from the date of instruction to recover a debt in full! Totally unreasonable, of course, but had the solicitor just taken the trouble to briefly explain to the client, at the outset, what was involved and the relevant time-scales, the complaint could have been totally avoided.

Another factor to bear in mind is that most people who consult a solicitor are under some degree of stress. They are in unfamiliar surroundings and have a problem that they would sooner not have and they are relying on someone else to solve it for them. What is more, they are having to pay for the privilege.

One characteristic that everyone subject to stress possesses is a short memory span, and the greater the stress, the shorter the span! What it means is that the solicitor must be meticulous in recording in writing everything that is of importance or significance to the client. A letter is ideal, but a file-note is better than nothing at all.

If this is not done, situations will frequently arise where the client is accusing the solicitor of not telling him something and the solicitor is protesting that he did – "I distinctly remember telling you that, and, anyway, I always tell my clients that." Well, a word of warning. The solicitor might be right and the client has just forgotten, but, if that complaint reaches the OSS, the solicitor will be expected to demonstrate that he did tell the client, which means producing some form of written evidence. If he can't do it, the client is going to get the benefit of the doubt.

There are precautions that can be taken to ensure that clients' expectations are being managed.

It is important that the terms of the retainer are put in writing and agreed by the client. Be careful, the wording of the letter needs careful drafting, bearing in mind that the courts are inclined to take a narrow view (*Hurlingham* v *Wilde & Partners* 1997 STC 627). If it isn't intended to advise on any aspect of the matter for which you are retained, you must say so clearly. The Hurlingham case concerned tax advice in a property transaction where the solicitor's defence was that he had agreed with the client that the client would seek any such advice from his accountant. The Judge, however, held that the solicitor, because he had not excluded it from the retainer, should still have advised his client if, and when, he needed to seek that advice.

Ask the client what they want and how they want it done. How can anyone start to properly advise a client unless they know what the client wants to achieve? In some cases it will be obvious – the client wants to move into his new house as soon as possible. In others it is not so clear. Using a divorce scenario, does your client want you to be aggressive and fight every last penny or does he want you to be conciliatory and negotiate an amicable settlement?

Next, don't presume or make assumptions – about anything! Too many solicitors think they know best and can completely disregard the client's views. Don't forget that in many cases, particularly divorce situations, the client will know the opponent far better than anyone else and will consequently very possibly have a better idea of the type of tactics which are likely to succeed. Ask if they have. Even if they haven't, or their ideas won't work (in which case, don't forget to explain why) – it gives the client much more of a feeling of being involved and part of what is going on.

Another aspect of this is:- how many divorce settlements, amicably agreed between the parties, have been wrecked by solicitors who have insisted the client should not accept what they themselves have freely agreed?

Naturally, for instance in a divorce situation, if you think the client really is settling at an under-valuation, they should be told that is your belief (and put it in writing) but if the client insists that is all they want, then why should the solicitor refuse to accept it (putting it in writing, of course, that he is going along with what the client wants against his better judgement)?

If you do otherwise, there are pitfalls for the unwary, particularly if, at the end of the day, the client, because of the imposition of extra costs involved in running the case, finds himself no better off, or, horror of horrors, even worse off, than had the original agreement been implemented. The unwary will then find themselves accused of running the case for their own benefit, not to mention the suggestion that the solicitor has wasted 18 months and achieved nothing better than was freely available 18 months earlier.

Some solicitors seem to perceive asking the client as a sign of weakness, suggesting they are incompetent in some way. What they are doing is making the error of perceiving technical excellence as replacing the client's needs and expectations. It is this confusion that is a contributory factor to the inappropriate way in which many solicitors deal with complaints. Indeed, the consequences of a solicitor giving a client what the solicitor perceives as first class treatment, without having understood what the client wants, can be quite bizarre.

The client comes to the conclusion that the solicitor has done much more than necessary and has milked the job for his own benefit. The resultant gap between what the client was expecting and the expense to them of what was provided will lead to them going elsewhere next time they need legal work doing.

Simply taking instructions to enable you to start work without knowing, for example, what level of non-legal service the client expects, can so easily lead to the client being alienated and perceiving the solicitor as being arrogant. For instance, does the client *really* want monthly progress reports; how fast do they expect responses to letters and telephone messages; do they expect the solicitor to be available outside normal office hours?

The answers to all these, and similar, questions are part of managing expectations and the answers can only be discovered by asking and informing.

Do not, ever, assume knowledge in a client. It doesn't matter how obvious you think something is, don't assume the client knows it. Check that he does.

Never assume people are who they say they are – even more essential now we have the money-laundering regulations with us.

Never assume that the person giving instructions on behalf of a company has the authority to do so.

Don't assume that clients accept that you are only instructed about matters they have mentioned to you. All too often they are expecting to be advised about any aspect of the matter under instruction. The solicitor may not be intending to advise on some aspect because he is not an expert in that particular field. Tax is the favourite. That is why it is essential to get the terms of the retainer right and precise.

If you take a file over from another firm, don't assume the first firm has explained everything to the client that they should have done and that they have done it in terms the client can understand. Check that it has been done.

Draw up an Action Plan in writing, telling the client what it is agreed you will do and the likely time scale for doing it.

In conveyancing, plans are a constant source of problems. It stems from the fact that when a solicitor produces a copy of a plan to a client, the client assumes that he is being given a guarantee that the plan accurately depicts the boundaries of the land he is buying. The lawyer cannot give that guarantee. All he is doing is guaranteeing the seller has title to what is shown on the plan and his client can safely take a transfer of it – and nothing more. Clients should, therefore, be told to check the accuracy of the plan for themselves and, if they have any doubts about it, it will mean that the client is probably going to have to employ a surveyor, at his own expense, to draw up an accurate plan, but that he should certainly be letting his solicitor know that he has doubts about the plan's accuracy.

What can be done about the anticipated troublesome client e.g. the one who comes in on a first appointment and proudly tells you they have already consulted four other solicitors on this and how useless they all were, and who is thereby announcing "I am likely to cause you so much grief you will be sorry you ever clapped eyes on me". Why do solicitors even contemplate accepting instructions from that type of person – they don't have to. Even if you would contemplate it, give yourselves a chance. Why not operate a free diagnostic interview? Tell the client that it is such and explain that you really don't know whether or not you can help him until you know more about the case and that *you will not be accepting them as clients until you are in a position to make a decision,* and will therefore not be charging them until the decision is made. That way you have a chance to assess whether this is someone who has just been plain unlucky to date or whether he is going to be more trouble than he is worth.

If you come to the conclusion that he falls into the latter category, you can always invent a reason why you cannot help and the "client" is less likely to feel aggrieved because it hasn't cost him anything. The impression can even be given that you really are trying to help him by suggesting he goes down the road to that firm you have been dying to get one across for months – they might well be able to assist!

# THE CAUSES OF COMPLAINT – THE USE OF JARGON

Much publicity has been given in recent years to plain English and encouragement given to practitioners to forsake their old ways and to draft documents using plain English. Things are getting better, but laymen still think that lawyers "speak in tongues" to maintain the mystique and justify large fees. It should constantly be born in mind that jargon, particularly in communications with the client, should be avoided like the plague. Remember also that what is everyday language for a lawyer is not necessarily so for the client. Indeed, it's sometimes very difficult for a solicitor to appreciate what is, or may be, jargon to a layman.

In March 2003 the Law Society published its Clients' Charter, one part of which assures clients that their solicitor will keep jargon to a minimum, and, in the supporting documentation, the Law Society gives examples of expressions which it says can amount to jargon to a layman. Such things as "vicarious liability", "forbearance" and even "codicil" are quoted as examples, and, of course, they are. Unfortunately, however, the problem is more deeprooted than that.

Basically, any word that has a specific legal meaning, even those in every day use, is still capable of being categorised as jargon and checks should be carried out to ensure that the solicitor and the client are talking about the same thing.

A stark example of this was provided by the case of a lady who complained to the OSS, explaining she had gone to a solicitor because she wanted to divorce her husband for adultery. She had given the solicitor the full names of the lady concerned, together with the exact date, time and place of the alleged adultery. The solicitor, impressed, no doubt, by the preciseness and the detail of the instructions, duly fired off a petition. When the solicitor received Answers stoutly denying the alleged adultery, he was somewhat perplexed and got the client in and began to probe more deeply into her account. Only then did it become clear that all that had happened was that the client and her husband had been to a party during which she had caught her husband in the kitchen kissing and fondling a neighbour. She genuinely thought that was adultery!!

The lesson is that you can never be too sure, even with words considered to be in common usage, particularly if they have a specific legal meaning. Who would have thought there was anyone who did not know what adultery was?

Ask any lawyer what "disbursements" are, and he would have no trouble in answering. Try going into the street and stopping the first person you meet and asking "Excuse me, can you tell me what disbursements are?" The answer could be quite interesting!

The same thing goes for expressions that a layman would not normally use. Even "hereinbefore referred to" is quite capable of being jargon to a layman. Certainly using expressions like "letters of the 7th ultimo" and "general and special damages" without explaining what they mean are jargon. Then there is the author's favourite – "discovery of documents". Lord only knows what the average layman thinks is meant by that!

Even worse, of course, is the use of Latin. Under no circumstances should Latin words or phrases be used in letters to clients – save them to impress other lawyers. The most common are "ex parte" and "prima facie", but other common examples are "sub judice", "in camera", "ex officio" and even "quantum" etc. The only exception to that general rule would be the use of "per stirpes" in a Will, but, even then, it should not just be included in the Will, but its use should be explained to the client both with regard to its meaning and why it is being used.

Equally objectionable are long or obscure words, such as "axiomatic", "para-doxical", "prescriptive" or "extrapolate". Such pleonasticity is not perspicuous. Your client will not thank you for pointing out that you are better educated than he, and he will certainly regard the use of such words as belittling.

Be on your guard at all times. In consultation the client may look at you very sagely and even nod as if he understands perfectly every word you are saying. You know, just like your dog does when you speak to him and he looks at you with bright eyes and pricked ears – "You know, I swear he understands every word I say". However, the dog doesn't and the chances are that neither does the client. Do check that, no matter what impression the client gives, he does really understand. People are often very diffident about saying they don't understand something in case they think it will make them look stupid, and do not like to appear stupid, so they keep quiet. It's only when things go wrong that you find out that they maintain that they never understood what was going on from the beginning. The position is even worse if it is written advice that is involved, because that needs a positive and pro-active effort by the client to say that he doesn't understand.

Assure clients that if there is anything that they don't understand, you want to be told. Clients cannot be expected to understand everything they are told first time and if you are told they don't understand something, then you can explain it in a way they will understand.

Remember that the advice you give should, as with costs information, be tailored to your individual client so that it is given in language that he can understand. If it isn't, you might as well not bother! Even when you think it has been understood, it is wise to check that it is.

## THE CAUSES OF COMPLAINT – COSTS INFORMATION

This is diminishing as a ground for complaint, but, for all that, still does form the grounds for a substantial proportion of complaints – about 14% of those reaching the OSS in 2003. The difference between today's complaints based on lack of costs information and those that used to be received lies in the type of information.

Although it became incumbent on members of the profession in 1991 to give the best information they could about costs at the outset of the retainer, it is only recently that most solicitors seem to have taken the requirement on board and complied with their obligations in that respect.

It was still apparent, however, that ongoing costs information was not being given as a matter of course and so the relevant provisions were tightened up when Rule 15 was revised, which Rule, in its revised form, took effect as from 3 September 1999. The nature of the Rule and its requirements are dealt with later, so only the areas that cause difficulty in this field will be dealt with at this point.

Most firms have cottoned on to the fact that they are supposed to give clients costs information at the outset of the retainer. However, still far too many cases arrive at the OSS where this has not been done, and caseworkers never cease to marvel at the ingenuity of the excuses offered by those who have not done so.

It is possible that the solicitor will get away with it – but only in a limited number of cases. And don't forget that, if costs information is not given and a complaint follows, the solicitor will be expected to justify the omission – the burden is on him.

Examples of circumstances that would justify such a failure would be taking repetitive (and I stress the word "repetitive" – not just "repeat") instructions from the same client. They would think you had taken leave of your senses if you started giving costs information every time a file was opened. Taking instructions for a death-bed Will, where it would be a little insensitive to give the impression all you were interested in was the money. Taking instructions from someone who was mentally disturbed and to whom, as a result, it could cause distress, or taking instructions in a domestic violence situation, where, if your costs letter was intercepted, it could cause difficulties for the client. However, there are very few others. Taking instructions in an emergency injunction matter might justify failing to give the information immediately, but there is no reason why it could not be done as soon as was reasonably possible.

And be warned. The general public are now aware that they are supposed to be given costs information at the outset of the matter and if the solicitor forgets, or fails to do so for whatever reason, they won't remind him, or ask. They keep quiet and when the bill is sent at the conclusion of the matter, they get in touch saying that they won't be paying it as the solicitor is not entitled to any costs as they had no costs information. Now, they are not right, but the solicitor now has the problem of extracting the money from the client and, if that complaint reaches the CCS, the solicitor is going to get his costs slashed by up 50%!

However, the main complaint these days is that clients have not been updated as to how costs are accumulating during the course of the retainer. There are some staggering examples of what has happened to firms who have not done this, none more so than the case, reported in the legal press in November 2002 which was heard in the Costs Court and which involved a very large City of London practice. They were ordered to repay to a client the staggering sum of £125,000 in costs because they had failed to update the client ever since they had given an initial costs estimate.

The whole subject of costs information, particularly in litigation, is a mine-field for the unwary practitioner, such are the ramifications and variations that it can involve.

One of the first questions the practitioner has to consider is when to give what amount of costs information.

It is entirely a matter for the individual firm, but it may be advisable to hesitate before trying to include every possible item of costs information in the client care letter unless it is extremely simple, such as a fixed fee quotation for a domestic Conveyancing matter, or a Will, or something similar.

Rule 15 does have all kinds of requirements with regard to costs information, but no-one can hope to cover all of them, for instance, in a civil litigation case, in a sensible and comprehensive way in a client care letter.

The danger lies in trying to put too much in the letter and, in trying to cover all eventualities, and subjecting the client to information overload. The client either forgets or he gets bored silly trying to make sense of information that has no meaning or relevance to him at that time. The problem is that if some-thing happens some time later that has a costs implication, the client has to be told then. If this is not done and he later complains, it is no use referring back to the original Client Care letter. Clients need to be told at the relevant time.

Even worse, something may be omitted that later turns out to be crucial and the solicitor forgets to tell the client about it because he thought he had already done so.

The dilemma is, how much information should be included?

One view is that any costs information in the client care letter should be restricted to the basic necessities. The firm should then work out standard clauses, in simple English, to cover all eventualities. These remaining matters can then be included in a separate, standard document with numbered paragraphs that can be given to the client, referring him at the outset to the specific relevant paragraphs. Then, as & when further paragraphs become applicable as the case progresses, the client can be referred to them by number. A variation on this which may be preferable is to give the document to all fee-earners and tell them that when the need to give costs information to a client arises, they use the relevant paragraph in the standard document.

If a Client Care letter is confined to the essentials as far as cost are concerned, the remainder can then be devoted to those other matters that Rule 15 demands, without the letter assuming gargantuan proportions. As well as information about the fee-earner and to whom the client can refer any concerns, the issues in the client's case can be confirmed, as can the clients instructions, any agreed plan of action and any relevant costs-risk/benefit factor that may have been discussed – all matters that Rule 15 requires.

Rule 15 requires the client be given "best information" and the Rule defines what that means. Obviously a fixed fee is ideal – if it can be done. But, if it cannot, the remainder of the definition can really be summed up by saying that the client should be told what the solicitor thinks it might cost. The whole purpose is that the client should not be taken by surprise when the solicitor eventually renders the bill.

If the solicitor gives the client his best guess as to what the costs are likely to amount to, updates that guess as and when necessary and also keeps the client regularly updated as to how costs are accumulating, he is fireproof.

A slight digression at this point, while on the subject of client care letters. There is not, and never has been, any obligation for a solicitor to send to a client a "client care letter". What Rule 15 and the Solicitors Costs Information & Client Care Code demand is that certain specified information must be given to the client in writing at the outset of the retainer.

Historically, what has happened is that, naturally, solicitors have always written a first letter to the client to confirm his instructions. When Rule 15 was first promulgated and began to require certain specific information to be given to the client, the obvious time to do it was when writing that first letter.

As the required information was classed as "client care" information, the quantum leap was then made to call that first letter a "client care letter" and to assume that it was compulsory to send one.

When the requirements began to be more comprehensive, it sparked loud and vociferous complaints from the profession about the fact that they were now being required to send "client care" letters to their clients which approached the length of "War & Peace". At the same time another myth was started – that solicitors now had to invite complaints from their clients or write to the client as if they expected him to complain.

In fact, Rule 15 only mentions the word "complaint" in connection with the requirement for a solicitor to operate an internal complaints handling procedure!

It would now be appropriate to examine in more detail the type and scope of costs information that a solicitor is expected to give to his client.

The requirements of Rule 15 with regard to costs are that clients are given the best information that they can be given with regard to the cost of legal services both at the outset of the matter and as it progresses. There are several ways in which this can be done. It should be noted, however, that whichever method is chosen, the information must be given in such a way that the individual client is capable of understanding it.

If a specific fee is not agreed, the client can still be given the solicitor's "best guess" as to what the costs are likely to amount to. It should be made absolutely clear to the client that that figure given is not fixed and might be more, or it might be less. However, assure the client that if it turns out that the "guesstimate" is not going to be high enough, he will be told immediately that becomes known he will be given an explanation.

Avoid relying on the word "estimate". Clients do not know the definition and they tend to regard any figure that is mentioned as a quotation, even if it is called something different.

There is one other piece of information that must be given, in writing, in every litigation case – a costs risk/benefit analysis. Do it in writing – it avoids arguments at a later date as to whether it was done at all, and, if it was, what was the view given. It need not be complicated. A simple sentence, if accurate will suffice eg "in my view the costs of the matter are likely to be justified by the end result".

If you have a client who is telling you that he only pursuing the case "as a matter of principle", be very sure that it is done. If it is not, a complaint when the bill is rendered can almost be guaranteed, with the client saying that if he had known at the outset what this was likely to cost, he would never have pursued it. He will be lying through his teeth, but the tragedy is that he is going to win this particular dispute. Put the analysis in writing and deny them the opportunity.

Clients should also be told the basis on which the bill will be calculated. This has been interpreted by many as meaning that all that is necessary in order to give clients adequate costs information is that the client is told the fee-earner's hourly charging rate and it is left at that. That is not, and, in fact, never has been, the case.

Nevertheless, due to the numbers who still give costs information solely in terms of hourly rates, a few words on that subject.

## HOURLY RATES

When giving costs information, there is a great temptation to quote an hourly rate with that being the sole information that is given. There are, of course, good reasons why that information has to be given in litigation matters, but please think twice before doing it if there is no good reason. It can be counter-productive!

Firstly the client thinks that the solicitor is working on the file all the time from inception to closure. He imagines all the hours that will involve and begins to imagine a bill arriving with a long row of noughts – it fosters the "fat cat" image. Clients also regard the whole thing as being open ended and at their risk. In addition, the solicitor now has no incentive to get the work done quickly and efficiently. Indeed, the opposite is regarded as the truth – the longer this takes, the more the solicitor will charge.

One thing to be avoided at all costs is to quote hourly rates with a separate mark up. A typical example would be – "my charge out rate is £150 per hour and in addition there will be a 50% mark-up for care & control". This kind of thing is an open invitation to a client to complain about the bill at a later date on the basis that he was given no care & control, so why should he pay for it? It also gives the impression that unless the client is prepared to pay extra, his job will be dealt with in any old slapdash fashion.

Perhaps the worst example of this was the firm who wrote, as recently as 2002, "Each fee-earner has a basic hourly expense rate which varies according to his or her experience and to which is added costs relevant to untimed letters and telephone calls, and a percentage uplift. This varies according to the nature of the matter, but is generally between 25 and 100%. It is not possible to calculate the precise uplift in any case until the matter is concluded. This is because it will depend on a number of factors which are listed in Appendix 2 to Order 62 of the Rules of the Supreme Court."

No doubt everyone can recite the provisions of the Order by heart, but even if they could, or, more importantly, even if the client could, what the client was being told, in effect, was that when the solicitor rendered his bill, he was going to think of a figure and he may double it!

A similar situation arose with another firm who, after quoting an hourly charging rate, told the client that it would be increased by up to 50% if one of nine factors applied. They then set out the factors, the last of which was the importance of the job to the client. Does anyone know of any client they have ever acted for who does not consider his job to be the most important that the solicitor has on at that particular time?

This points up the big problem with merely quoting hourly rates. That is, they are absolutely meaningless unless the client is also given an idea of how long, in terms of hours of work, the matter is likely to take. Without giving such an estimate of time, how can the client be getting "best information"?

Nevertheless, if costs information is given in this way (or even if it is not for that matter), it must be remembered that the client should be told if, and when, hourly rates may be increased – and it must also be remembered to tell them when that happens, what the new rate is and what effect it may have on the overall estimate if one has been given.

This is also an opportunity for the practitioner to dispel another of those myths that the general public has about the legal profession.

That is to say, the belief that the longer a case takes to complete, the more the solicitor is going to be paid and it is, therefore, in his interest to prolong matters for as long as possible. Explain to the client that you are only paid for the work actually done; that if a job actually takes five hours work to achieve the desired result, it does not matter whether that five hours is spread over five hours, five days, five months or five years, you are still only going to be paid the same amount and it is, therefore, contrary to popular belief, in your interests to get the job done as quickly as possible.

# COSTS INFORMATION IN LITIGATION MATTERS

The area in which most complaints of inadequate costs information arises is Civil Litigation, which is a veritable minefield for the unwary. For that reason, this section will concentrate on that area of work.

For a start, how many solicitors appreciate all the various ways in which litigation can be funded? It is instructive to consider the possibilities, even without going into great detail.

Firstly, consider private paying clients. They can be charged on an hourly basis or on a fixed fee basis, which may become increasingly the norm as a result of fast-track cases and the imposition of fixed fees in various fields of contentious work. Then there are other possibilities starting to emerge, for example, the possibility of minimum/maximum fee arrangements being imported from the USA.

Then there are Contingency arrangements.

Although contingency fees as such, whereby the solicitor receives a share of the damages in successfully prosecuted cases, are still illegal in this country in litigation cases, it would seem that this arrangement is increasingly used in non-contentious matters by means of Non-Contentious Business Agreements. These can be used, for example, in Employment Tribunal cases or CICB claims.

Perhaps here would be an appropriate place to digress slightly in order to clear up another issue that seems to cause an inordinate amount of confusion among solicitors, that is to say, what is, and what is not, Contentious or Non-Contentious work.

Basically all work in which proceedings are issued is contentious, including work done before the issue of proceedings but carried out specifically with a view to the issue of proceedings and where proceedings are actually issued as a result.

This, however, as the legal world loves exceptions, does not include proceedings before Tribunals, with the exception of the Lands Tribunal and the Employment Appeals tribunal, and proceedings before Public Inquiries.

Everything else is non-contentious work.

The concept of Conditional Fees extends, as from 30 July 1998, to all civil litigation except family matters.

The essential element of this is that the solicitor gets no fees if the case is lost and, if it is won, the fees are an hourly rate enhanced by a success fee with a maximum enhancement of 100%. The Law Society recommends that the success fee should not normally exceed 25% of the damages recovered.

Conditional fee insurance is available to provide cover against the risk of having to pay the opponents fees and the client's own disbursements should the case be lost and, although not mandatory by law, is required as a condition under various schemes, such as Accident Line Protect.

Then there is the question of Contingent Fees.

The Access to Justice Act refers to this arrangement as "conditional fees without enhancement" ie a success fee. In effect it means the solicitor gets his ordinary fees (whatever that may mean) if the case is won and nothing if it is lost. This type of arrangement will probably not be attractive except in the case of acting for close family and friends or when pro bono work is being done.

Then there is Legal Expense Insurance, together with funding by an institution such as a Trade Union. One also then has to consider two other types of Insurance that are available – General Liability Insurance and After the Event Insurance.

Finally there is still the possibility of Public Funding, either with, or without, a contribution, although it disappeared for most money claims as from April 2000. Nevertheless, where it is still available, remember the client still needs protecting against the payment of disbursements and the possibility of a costs order against him.

Make enquiries to see if the client is eligible for public funding or carries, or can get, legal expense insurance. Record the enquiry and answer in writing – it could be difficult at a later date to show you have done this otherwise.

Remember also that if a client is eligible for public funding and the firm doesn't do it, that the client must be so advised and told that, if he wishes to do so, he can go elsewhere to someone that does.

Remember to indicate whether any figure given is inclusive or exclusive of VAT and disbursements, being careful, as previously stated, to distinguish between an estimate and a quotation and making sure that the client understands the difference, and if a right is being reserved to increase the figure given, that that is made clear to the client.

# ESSENTIAL COSTS INFORMATION IN LITIGATION MATTERS

This is perhaps the area which gives practitioners the most problems. This does, however now form part of the requirements of the new Rule 15, and so will be dealt with in more detail.

Remember, there are at least six things a potential litigant should always be told *before proceedings are commenced* – and most of them also apply to defendants before a defence is filed. After all, the client may, armed with the knowledge of what it might cost him, to decide to swallow his pride and pay up.

The first five of the six are relatively easy to spot, but the last is not and is a trap for the unwary. The six are:-

1.  The client will have to pay some of his solicitor's costs even if he is 100% successful and the court makes an order for his costs to be paid by the other party. This is now even more important than it used to be as Courts can now make partial costs orders and there is the increased likelihood of tariffs being applied that can mean that even a successful client may find there is a significant difference between his own costs and those he can recover from his opponent.

2.  notwithstanding an order that the other party is to pay his costs, the client is still primarily responsible for meeting his own solicitor's bill, and any monies the solicitors receive, whether in respect of damages or otherwise, will be firstly applied to meeting that liability and only when their bill has been paid will the client get anything himself.

3.  a court order to the effect that his opponent has to pay him damages and/or costs does not mean that the client will automatically get his money.

4.  in addition to 3. above, the costs of taking enforcement proceedings to obtain payment of any monies due under a court order will form a separate retainer (jargon!) and will be in addition to any costs involved in pursuing the actual proceedings.

5.  the potential liability to the client, if he loses the case, with regard to his opponent's costs and those of any other party to the proceedings.

6.  is the price of withdrawal from the proceedings if, for any reason, the client decides he does not want to go on. This is a trap because there is another requirement of Rule 15 i.e. that the client can, if he wishes, put a ceiling on costs. What this means is that if, for instance, the client says he is happy to spend £4,000 on his case, but doesn't want to spend any more, he must be told, before he ever starts the proceedings, that he may only be able to spend half that sum on his own case. If he then wants to withdraw,

he may be required to pay the other half to his opponent as the price of withdrawal. It also means that the solicitor must keep an eye on how costs are accumulating and tell the client, not when the costs are approaching £4,000, but when they are approaching £2,000.

In addition, if there is ANY possibility of the opponent becoming legally-aided, there is a seventh, which is that a solicitor should inform the client of the implications, as far as costs recovery is concerned, of that happening, and the knock-on effect it has on the client's liability to pay his own costs.

If the client is, or becomes, legally aided, there are five more. There must be explained to him:-

A.  the nature and effect of the statutory charge, and in language the client will understand eg this is a loan, not a gift, and, like most other loans, it becomes repayable in the event that the client wins his case and, as a result, either obtains money or property, or retains money or property, which is being claimed in the proceedings.

B.  that before the client will receive any money, the solicitor will have to send all money received to the Legal Services Commission, so they can recoup any part of the loan due to it.

C.  the effect of any later discharge or revocation of the Certificate and what the causes are. Remember that the client may not be asked to repay costs due to the Legal Services Commission for some considerable time afterwards and he should be warned that it could be months, or even years before the demand is made.

D.  if an interim payment is made, that, although that payment is exempt from the statutory charge, should the balance payable at the end of the case be insufficient to meet the Charge, the client will have to meet the difference. i.e. he may have to cough up the relevant part of the interim payment

E.  the solicitor's duties to the Legal Services Commission (and to Legal Expense Insurers) to report the situation to it if the outlook with regard to a successful conclusion to the case changes for the worse and that the Legal Services Commission (or the Insurers) may then withdraw their support. Time and again the CCS receives complaints that a solicitor has sabotaged the client's case by procuring the withdrawal of his public funding, and all because the solicitor has failed to give the appropriate warning to the client when public funding was applied for and again when the decision was taken that the changed prospects had to be reported.

Clients must understand clearly that when they first instruct their solicitor, the advice that he will give about the chances of success are based entirely on the information the client gives him. He knows nothing about what the other side may say, and what they say may alter his views. In every piece of litigation there are two sides who both think they are going to succeed – there would be no litigation otherwise. It follows, therefore, that the other side may come up with information that the client does not have and cannot anticipate. This may dramatically alter the solicitor's perception of the chances of success.

In all matters don't forget to explain *fully* the implications of a payment into court. Don't forget to say, as has been done on more than one occasion, that if the client fails to beat the amount paid in, he will have to pay, not just his opponent's costs from the date of the payment in, but also his own as well. If, in a legally aided case, an interim payment is sought, that payment is exempt from the statutory charge, so the client needs to be told that if what he gets back at the end of the day in addition to the statutory charge is insufficient to meet the statutory charge ie. to repay the loan, the LSC will expect him to repay the necessary part of the interim payment to satisfy the Charge.

Remember also to tell the client:- at regular intervals, what costs have accrued. This is best done by rendering interim bills at not less than 6 monthly intervals, and preferably more frequently as soon as it is known that the solicitor is going to want to increase an estimate, or an agreed costs limit, is likely to be exceeded any other relevant information about costs risk or liability as & when it becomes appropriate.

ALSO REMEMBER THAT ALL COSTS INFORMATION SHOULD BE CONFIRMED IN WRITING by one means or another.

A case illustrating the potential problems occurred where a solicitor was obviously, and perhaps accurately, anticipating a complaint.

He had accepted instructions in a case where he, quite reasonably, anticipated a 100% success. There are no certainties in litigation, but this was as close as anyone is ever going to get to that situation. The client's car had been parked outside his house and was hit by another driver. The solicitor didn't intend charging the client any costs and was going to be content with the costs he was able to recover from the third party insurers. Because of that, he didn't send out a client care letter.

It transpired the client had unreasonable expectations about how quickly the claim could be progressed and, before it could be concluded, transferred his instructions to another firm who duly requested the file.

The solicitor had then raised a bill and sought to exercise his right to a lien on the papers.

The solicitor had to be advised that if his intention not to charge his client was founded on the expectation that he would handle the case from start to finish, then he should have said so, in writing, at the outset. He was entitled to raise a bill and exercise his lien, but, if the client complained and the complaint came to the CCS, the bill would certainly be reduced, or even cancelled, and it was suggested to him that it might be wise for him to consider coming to some agreement with the new solicitors whereby he would be paid at the end of the case for the work he had done.

Finally, and this applies to ALL contentious matters. It is part of the Protocol, but so often seems to be ignored. Before going to court for the final hearing, a solicitor should work out, fairly accurately, the amount of the costs to date, and include any costs of which he is aware, eg counsel's, or expert's, fees for attending court. That way, if a settlement is proposed, he will be able to work out much more readily what effect proposals as to costs will have on the proposed settlement. The CCS receives countless complaints where the client settled a case at court, only to find that what he actually received fell way below the amount he was expecting to receive, the reason being because he was given, at best, inaccurate information about the amount of costs the client would have to meet.

When the case has concluded it may well now be necessary to remind the client of those matters of which he was advised before the case started that may now be relevant because he will have forgotten what he was told at the outset. In addition, if the ability to account to the client is going to be hampered by the necessity of having costs assessed, a client must be told what this entails and how long it is likely to take. Many complaints arise from the client's impression that the solicitor is holding onto his money for no valid reason.

## ADDITIONAL COSTS INFORMATION IN OTHER DISCIPLINES

In Divorce matters, practitioners should ensure that the client understands, if he is being given a quote for a simple divorce *that this does not include ancillary matters*. Every solicitor knows very well that the two are quite separate considerations. Clients do not. Normally, when a client talks of "divorce", he is referring to all things connected with it, and, unless he is told otherwise, will assume that the quote he has been given will apply to everything. And solicitors need to beware of referring to "ancillary matters" – that is jargon again!

In Conveyancing matters, if the solicitor intends charging the client should the matter prove to be abortive, he must ensure that the client knows that and how the fee is going to calculated.

If the solicitor reserves the right, when giving a quote, to increase his fee should the matter turn out to be more complicated than he had thought, he must ensure that the client is told IMMEDIATELY he knows that he is going to want to invoke that right. He should explain to the client what are the reasons and by how much it is thought the fees will be increased.

One further matter relative to costs in all types of matter. Do discuss at an early stage, preferably at the first meeting, how the client is going to pay the bill and when interim bills will be sent. That information can then be confirmed in the client care letter.

Also, unless it is already the case, consider taking credit cards. It can make it very difficult for the client to refuse a payment on account if he is told he can pay by credit card.

# CHAPTER TWO

# COMMUNICATION: A COMMON CAUSE OF COMPLAINT

## DELAY AND FAILING TO INFORM THE CLIENT

It might, at first sight, appear odd to place these two causes of complaint together under one head, however, hopefully, all will become clear.

If anyone wants convincing of the effects of failing to tell clients about things that the solicitor considers of minor importance, they can do no better than to have a look at the Case Study that appeared in the 29 January 2004 edition of the *Gazette*. It highlights the dangers of a solicitor perceiving an event as being commonplace and routine and therefore of no interest to the client. This is because the solicitor is looking at matters entirely from his own point of view and failing to appreciate the client's viewpoint.

Remember that very little will be commonplace and of no interest to the client. It is therefore vitally important that, no matter how busy a practitioner may be, no matter how much pressure he is under, that he keeps clients informed even about matters that he considers to be of little interest or significance.

One of the most common complaints nowadays is that of delay. In point of fact, on investigation, it often turns out that the complaint should be one of failing to keep the client informed. These two together, delay and a failure to keep the client informed, account for about 40% of the complaints currently received by the CCS.

The confusion arises from the fact that clients can only put complaints as they perceive them. Remember, they know little or nothing, of legal procedures. The result is that it is quite easy for a client who is unhappy to get the wrong idea of what is the cause of his problem – and this is the most common example.

There are often situations that arise that inevitably result in the progress of the case being delayed, but the problem is that the solicitor has forgotten to tell the client. A good example is where a solicitor knows that before any further progress can be made, a specialist medical report is needed. It is well known that it is an unfortunate fact that it can sometimes be months before this is made available. Under such circumstances the solicitor should enquire whether it is possible for the specialist to give an estimate of how long it will take for him to examine the client and then to produce his report. The client can then be told that he will not hear from the solicitor again until the report is to hand, at which time he will be sent a copy for agreement, and that is not likely to be for the period of time indicated by the specialist.

Let us assume that the solicitor knows that a report is likely to take four months. He can write to the client explaining this and saying he will send a copy as soon as the report is to hand. He can then forward diary the matter for four months. After four months have elapsed, if he still hasn't received the report, he can now write to the client telling him the report has not arrived but that he is chasing it. This has two effects. Firstly, and most importantly, the client is getting the message that clients constantly want – 'I haven't been forgotten'. Secondly, the client knows his solicitor is "on the ball".

Consider what happens if this is not done. From the client's point of view, he has not heard from his solicitor for four months. In his mind this means that nothing has been done for four months which equates to the solicitor delaying the progress of his case. When he then complains, his complaint is likely to be one of delay. There is then a great temptation for the solicitor to respond by saying 'I know nothing has happened for four months, but it's not my fault – I'm waiting for that report' – and he dismisses the complaint. This does nothing to assuage the client who now thinks he is being fobbed off. And, of course, in a sense, he is. He picked the wrong thing to complain about, but he knew no better and could do little else.

It is even worse if, in fact, the solicitor has been working flat out on the file for four months and has simply neglected to tell the client. The indignant response to the complaint then is likely to be 'what does this man want, blood?' and to regard him as a trouble-maker who is never going to be satisfied.

Other instances where the same situation will arise will readily spring to mind.

If the client is not warned, the result is that he will conclude that his case has been forgotten and is being neglected. Any such conclusion is only reinforced if another situation which commonly gives rise to complaints also occurs, i.e. a failure to take or return telephone calls, these commonly being made as a result of the client not having heard anything for some time without any explanation being given.

Once the client concludes the solicitor has lost interest, the solicitor, in turn, has lost the client. The conclusions the client has reached may be totally wrong and, in fact, plenty may have been going on, but whatever the client is told once the complaint has been made, no matter how justified it may be, will be regarded as an excuse and not a reason.

One excuse that will certainly not be acceptable, either to the client or the CCS, is pressure of work. If a solicitor takes on so much work that he cannot cope, that is his problem, not the client's.

Active steps must be taken to keep the client informed. Regular updates must be sent unless it has been agreed, in writing, that they are not required.

Solicitors must take care to ensure that they do not to get so involved with arguing interesting and complicated points with the other side that the fact that there is a client out there, anxiously wanting to know what is happening, is totally forgotten.

Everyone should ensure that they have in place a regular reporting and brought-forward system and, because any system is dependent on humans to work it (even a computerised system needs the information putting into it), and is therefore not infallible, ensure that time is found to carry out a regular trawl of files as well.

## KEY AREAS RELATING TO DELAY/FAILING TO INFORM THE CLIENT

### General reporting

You must ensure you have a system, in all cases, to report progress on a regular basis or at identified stages. A common complaint is that the client was never told what was going on and, if he ever wanted to know, he always had to contact the solicitor and ask. Give the client a brief update at not more than two monthly intervals. Advise the client of any significant event.

Similarly report any change in direction etc. Clients may not know all the technicalities involved in their case, but usually they do have a good idea where their case is going and if it suddenly starts heading off in another direction without explanation, they tend to get anxious and annoyed. In conveyancing matters, a lot of trouble could be saved by supplying to the client copies of relevant documents.

Also remember to use straightforward language and to be brief.

### Costs

These have, of course, been dealt with as a separate issue earlier.

### Changes in procedure/personnel

Don't forget that one of the requirements of Rule 15 is that a client should know the name and status of the person dealing with his case. That does not just mean at the outset of the matter. It is an ongoing requirement. If there is a change, write saying who will be dealing with the matter in future and confirming their status and explaining the reason for the change and any amendment to the charge-out rate if that is applicable.

The other issue is to ensure that the firm has a workable monitoring system in place. Any reporting system should be capable of being checked – everyone makes mistakes. Regular file checks should be made and ensuring that a report has been sent to the client should form part of that check.

There is a great temptation to dismiss trawling as time consuming, particularly by the busy practitioner who is under pressure. It needn't be so, and, if the firm's professional indemnity insurers know that a firm does this as a matter of course, they are likely to fall round the firm's neck with delight as it would save so many negligence claims.

Even with a computerised filing and brought-forward system, the scope for error is there. It depends on the fee-earner putting the brought-forward date into the computer. It's easy to see how this can be missed. The fee-earner is working on a file and thinks 'if nothing else happens on that, I must look at it again in two weeks time'. He is just about to enter the brought-forward date in the computer when the telephone goes and he is on to another client, another file. When that call is finished he completely forgets that he never actually got round to entering the brought-forward date in the computer. Both files go back in the cabinet, and there the first one stays until the negligence writ hits the desk. (Some computerized systems have now built in failsafes on this – but don't assume yours has!)

What makes trawling so time consuming is the necessity of getting the file out of the cabinet, opening it up, reminding oneself what it is all about, what one did last and what is the next thing to do. If we can cut that out, we have won – and it can be done.

It means having a paper diary. This is really a back-up. When the brought-forward date is put into the computer, write the file reference on the same date in the diary. Now, if the computer crashes, at least the fee-earner knows what he was supposed to be looking at on that day. If the computer is used to remind the fee-earner of limitation periods, this is essential. But the important thing is that that date is now written in the top outside corner of the file cover. If something else happens and the date is altered, cross the date out and write in another. Now, when the fee-earner wants to do his trawl, he doesn't even have to get the file out of the cabinet – he just pulls it far enough to see the date. If it is a date in the future, he puts the file back. After all, he has already made a conscious decision once that that is the next date he needs to look at that file. If it is a date in the past, it has slipped the system and he gets it out and does something with it.

Using that method, the author found it possible to trawl over 350 files in 30 minutes!

# A FAILURE TO REPLY

Failing to reply to letters and telephone calls speaks for itself. It is the most common cause of all complaints in the sense that it is the catalyst that provokes heads of complaint that would not otherwise have arisen had the client's communications been answered.

The problem with *letters* usually arises when solicitors take too long to reply, particularly if the letter is in response to one from the client and demands of a long, complicated letter of advice that the solicitor knows is going to take him some time to dictate, and he has so much on that he knows he won't be able to do it for another two weeks at least.

If that kind of thing happens, send a letter of acknowledgement to the client so he knows the solicitor has received his letter. In it explain the reason why it is unlikely that a full response can be provided within the next 14 days (allow a day or so longer than it is anticipated will be required) but assure the client that it will be dealt with just as soon as it is possible to do so.

Now, the client is not likely to be entirely happy with that, but, if it is left for 14 days without any word at all, he will be whole lot unhappier.

Clients tend to have their own schedule and it runs something like 'one day for my letter to get to my solicitor. Another day for him to reply and another day for his letter to get to me.' It means that, on the fourth morning after posting his letter, the client is sitting behind his front door waiting for the postman to come with the reply. When it doesn't arrive, he is a little disappointed. He is there again the next morning, and when it doesn't arrive then, he is even more disappointed. With every day that goes by, that sense of disappointment deepens until it starts to change into anger.

On the twelfth day, when the letter does finally arrive, instead of the client's reaction being 'Oh, good, that's sooner than he said. Let's have a look what he's got to say', the reaction is likely to be 'And about time too. What is this man playing at? Why is he taking so long?'

If a client asks a number of questions, please give an answer to them all, even if the answer is 'I'm sorry, I don't know – but I'll try to find out and if I can I'll tell you.'

Too often practitioners just seem to omit to answer a question, perhaps through embarrassment that they don't know the answer and they don't want to admit it to the client. However, the client just gets angry because he thinks he is just being ignored.

Most commonly, it is telephone calls that are the problem.

There is nothing that infuriates clients as much as the failure of solicitors to return telephone calls when asked to do so, or when they are told it will be done.

The solicitor does not return a call – the client is annoyed and calls again. If this one is also missed the relationship is just about doomed. The client gets the impression, rightly or wrongly that the solicitor is avoiding him. His calls get more and more insistent. The solicitor starts to regard the client as being more and more of a nuisance. Their relationship is on the inevitable path to self-destruction and the client now starts to find a whole raft of other things to complain about, that probably would not have occurred to him had his call been returned in the first place.

Every practice should ensure it has a system in place that ensures that every telephone call is recorded, a note is made, that the intended recipient of the call gets the note and that he then deals with it, no matter how much he may not like doing so. And a note of both the incoming call and a note of the return call should be put on the file.

If a call cannot be returned by the fee-earner, for whatever reason, the solicitor's secretary should ring back, explain why and say when the return call will be made. And this should be done as a matter of course without the secretary waiting to be told to do so. The call should be made, explaining to the client why the fee-earner cannot do so and arranging a mutually convenient time when the call can be made. It is essential that a note of both the incoming call and a note of the return call should be put on the file. Even if the client's phone is engaged when the return call is made, make a note on the file.

Typical of a complaint that would reach the CCS would be "I rang my solicitor ten times in November. I could never get to speak to him, but he never once rang me back, even though I was told he would do so." That complaint is sent to the solicitor and the response can often be anticipated – "We have no trace of any of these calls being made." That response is sent to the client who now plays his trump card. It is called an itemised telephone bill with the solicitor's number highlighted ten times in November. Guess who gets the benefit of the doubt!

It is, in fact, your support staff (your telephonist or secretary) who can be of immense value in such matters because it is they who will usually detect the first signs of a complaint of this nature beginning to grow and, consequently, they can play a vital role – provided the solicitor also plays his part.

The client makes a telephone call and the solicitor is not available to take it. The telephonist offers to take the caller's name and number and says the solicitor will call the client. If she gets a retort like "If he does, it will be the first time" or "You can try – wonders never cease" there is a complaint in the making – and the fee-earner should be told. When told, it is essential that he immediately does something about it. Probably all that is needed at that stage is a call to the client, apologising for the other calls that were not returned and giving an assurance that it will not happen again.

For the clients who are a genuine nuisance and who persist in making daily calls, or even multiple unwarranted calls per day, provided that proper costs information has been given, usually a gentle reminder that calls cost money and that you are having to charge for the calls will do the trick. Even if the client is publicly funded, a reminder that public funding is in the nature of a loan and that the client will end up paying in the long run, will prove effective.

Do remember at all times that what really upsets people more than anything else is not having information. If you relate that to your own circumstances and day-to-day situations in which you find yourselves, you will realise how true that is.

It is this failure to reply to telephone calls that are frequently the cause of the monster complaints that arrive. Because clients get infuriated about failure to return calls, they begin to light on all the other little things that have niggled them about the relationship with their solicitor – and they blow those up in their own minds into full scale complaints. They even, sometimes, go so far as to start inventing things that have actually never happened, but they convince themselves they have and these are added in also. If you are ever called upon to deal with a monster complaint that seems to just be so much repetitive rubbish, just have a look and see if, in the middle of it all, there isn't a suggestion that the client's telephone calls have not been returned. Very often it will be there.

## THE BASIC REQUIREMENT

All that has been said can be summed up in one word – communication.

There are no exact figures available, nor does there appear to be any research specifically on the subject, but a reasonable estimate is that at least 90% of all complaints have poor communications as their root cause. For a profession in which the use of words is a basic requirement, its communication with clients is, generally speaking, sadly lacking.

The Customer Management Consultancy, in their Report to the Law Society, quoted Professor Clark Cunningham of Washington University, St Louis, who said that there was "considerable concern that failures of communication create dissatisfaction and undermine reputation as well as fundamental principles of justice."

University of the West of England research in 1996/7 concluded "Good communication will help clients receive services that match their needs and expectations, know what is being done for them and approximately how much it will cost. For solicitors...good communication ensures they are aware of the specific needs of clients and can recognise and address problems speedily should these occur".

The problem is that there is still a significant sector of the profession that believes that "because I am a qualified solicitor, I know best and the client should just accept what I do without question or the need for explanation". That attitude is a root cause of an enormous number of complaints that are levied against the profession.

And remember that communications need to be clear. The client needs to be able to understand what he is being told. Otherwise one may as well not bother.

## A FINAL WORD

If you are unfortunate enough to be subjected to delayed flights when you are going on holiday, what is it about that that irritates you more than anything else? Would it be very wide of the mark to suggest that almost everyone would say that it is being kept in the dark and not being told what is the nature of the problem that is causing the delay and not being given any idea about when the problem is expected to be resolved?

It is the same with clients.

A delayed flight may be extremely annoying, but the aggravation may well be dissipated to a large extent if only one knew what the problem was. After all, very few people would opt to fly in a plane knowing that one of the engines was not working!

If solicitors would just bear that in mind and treat clients in the way that they, themselves, would like to be treated in such circumstances, the distinct possibility is that an enormous number of complaints could be avoided altogether.

# CHAPTER THREE
# CAUSES OF COMPLAINTS IN INDIVIDUAL DISCIPLINES

## CIVIL LITIGATION

The main areas of complaint in civil litigation matters are:

- not keeping the client abreast of what is going on. Experience would suggest that, whatever may be the reason, there is a greater likelihood of this happening in civil litigation than in any other type of work

- the way a client perceives his case is being conducted without his participation. The fact is that clients *do* want to be involved with their own matters. They are likely to get very upset if they perceive that their case is being conducted without their views and input. Of course they will look to their professional adviser for advice and guidance, and the solicitor will be able to guide the client down the path along which he judges it best to go. But that does not mean the client wants to be told which way he is going to go. He wants to feel that the decision is a joint one in which his views are taken into account

- clients being advised to accept settlements without discussion or even consideration of their views. Clients sometimes have optimistic ideas about what they are likely to recover, but, remember chapter one and managing a client's expectations?

- delay in the client being paid out his damages, particularly where there is a dispute about costs due to the solicitor, or account has to be made to the Legal Services Commission

- lack of advice about the accumulation of costs. All that needs to be said about that subject has already been covered in the relevant part of the chapter on The Cause and Characteristics of a Complaint, but it is as well to emphasise that complaints on this subject continually reach the CCS. In fact they are complaints that should never see the light of day and would not do so if only practitioners took care to recognise when a development in the case had an implication that could have a financial effect on the client and then took the trouble to ensure that those implications were *fully* explained

- allowing claims to be struck out under automatic provisions. This is not strictly something for the CCS or for a solicitor to deal with under the firm's internal complaints procedure, unless the claim is for a specifically identifiable sum less than £5000 (or the firm's insurance excess) or the claim is reinstated etc, in which case it would be dealt with as a complaint of delay.

## DIVORCE

There are seven main pitfalls in matrimonial cases.

### 1. Failing to "finish off" the job

It is a curious fact, and a puzzling one, but a surprising number of solicitors, for some reason or another, just simply fail to complete the work in a divorce matter. They seem to think that, once they have got an order that ties up all the ancillary claims, that is it. Either nothing more is done to give effect to the order or it is done at a very leisurely pace.

Perhaps it is the mental relief of having got the hard work out of the way so that there is a feeling of relaxation about the matter, or perhaps it is overwork and the practitioner feels under pressure to get on with something else.

Whatever may be the reason, one thing is for sure – whatever the solicitor may think, the client, quite rightly, does not consider the job to be finished until effect has been given to the Order which has been obtained.

Consider the following, perfect, example. In this case, it was not the Ancillary Order that was not finished off, but the actual divorce itself. It also highlights the fact that the solicitor in question did not have a proper reminder system, or, if he did, he was not using it. Incidentally, it is also a perfect illustration of a solicitor being dismissive in the handling of a perfectly valid complaint.

The solicitors had acted for a wife in a divorce matter and everything had proceeded quite satisfactorily. The solicitors were instructed in March, a petition was issued in May with Decree Nisi in August. Financial matters were dealt with in a Consent Order on 1 September and, on 15 September the solicitors wrote to their client saying they would be applying for Decree Absolute in two days time i.e. 17 September. They forgot. Fourteen months later the client, wishing to remarry, was told by the Registry Office that she needed her Decree Absolute and, not knowing any better, she approached the court for a copy. It was then that she learned to her dismay that there had never been an application made.

She contacted the solicitors on 23 November, and having heard nothing, faxed them on 27 November asking for an explanation of why they had failed to apply for Decree Absolute, saying she felt shocked and emotionally distressed when she discovered she was still married when she had thought she had been divorced for over a year. In fact, the solicitors had obtained the Decree Absolute two days earlier (although how they had been able to give the necessary declaration that the client had not given birth between Decree Nisi and Decree Absolute was never explained) and had posted it to the client, but it was delayed in the course of delivery.

The solicitor's response to the complaint of 27 November was astonishing. It read "I cannot comment as to why Decree Absolute was not applied for. It is, however, not automatic. There is no question of negligence. If somebody wanted to get married and get Decree Absolute, it is a simple thing to get the document from the court. I am sorry you have taken this so amiss. Do you want me to get the file up?"

The client's reaction, which was, perhaps, predictable, was to accuse the solicitors of being callous, arrogant and dismissive – and was that any surprise? There was not even an apology, except for a rather offhand one – certainly no expression of regret that the application had been overlooked.

Her reaction could, perhaps, have been expected. She wrote "I find (the) comment that 'I have taken this so amiss' in very poor taste at the least. I am entitled to an explanation and at the very least an apology for the distress this has caused me. Instead he seems to be trying to justify his lack of attention to detail."

Perhaps the solicitor's attitude which resulted in his seeming lack of sympathy can be gauged from a letter he subsequently wrote to the OSS when he said "(I) cannot possibly see the reasons for complaint, insofar as the matter was immediately rectified. If clients complained about every single thing that happened of a minor nature, then the writer is not surprised (the OSS gets so many complaints)".

Sometimes one is lost for words!

## 2. Conflict situations

Such circumstances occur when the solicitor finds himself acting for both parties i.e. the husband and wife – or what is euphemistically known as a common-law husband and wife. The situation can be tricky enough when both parties are agreed on what they want to achieve, but, if there is *any* degree of discord, there can easily be trouble ahead, and if they at each other's throats, there is a disaster just waiting to happen. And, in matrimonial situations, the scope for problems to arise is simply unlimited.

Even in situations where the parties *are* genuinely in agreement, do not be lulled into a false sense of security. Things can change, and, if they do, there are problems ahead, usually with a capital "P". Take the example of the husband and wife who were in complete agreement that the former matrimonial home had to be sold, and they were also agreed that the proceeds should be split evenly. Then they started to bicker over points that certainly had no relevancy to the house, and precious little relevancy to anything else either. The sale was completed and the husband, seeking to "put one over" on his wife then instructed the solicitors that there was a dispute about the division of the proceeds. There wasn't – the husband just wanted to inconvenience the wife – and he succeeded. The solicitors, no doubt prompted by caution, withheld the proceeds, leading to an inevitable complaint from the wife.

Don't make rash assumptions. Just because similar instructions are received from both parties, don't assume, in a relationship break-down situation, that they both want the same thing. Don't even make that assumption if there is a Court Order in existence that dictates that the property shall be sold.

The kind of thing that can so easily happen, even when the parties appear to be in agreement, was illustrated in case where a solicitor was acting for both parties, who had separated, in the sale of the former matrimonial home. It was known that the wife intended to apply for a Property Adjustment Order and it was therefore agreed that the solicitors should hold the net proceeds of sale until that matter was resolved. However, on completion day the husband refused to vacate the house unless he got 50% of the net proceeds and the solicitors, no doubt influenced by the pressure exerted by a chain of furniture vans in transit around the country, acceded to his demands.

Care must be taken that practitioners do not find themselves unwittingly acting for both parties. In a case that reached the OSS the solicitors concerned had acted for the husband in a divorce matter, with the wife being separately represented. It was agreed that the house should be sold and the proceeds divided equally. There was an Ancillary Relief claim current and, after completion, the solicitors, suspicious that the wife was not being entirely frank about disclosure in the Ancillary Relief claim, withheld her share of the sale proceeds in an attempt to force her to full disclosure of her means. When the wife complained, the solicitor's response was that she was not their client, but the OSS decided that on the facts of that particular matter, as far as the sale was concerned, she was and that the solicitors who were acting for her in the divorce were not acting in the sale – they were merely used as a useful conduit for passing on documentation etc. It must be said that, in that case, the solicitor's argument that they were not acting for the wife was not assisted by the fact that their bill for the sale was made out against both the husband and wife!

The lesson is that solicitors must beware of getting themselves into a situation where they end up acting for both parties on the sale of a jointly owned former matrimonial home. This situation is a complaint waiting to happen – and when it does, it is not just a matter of inadequacy of service, it is usually a conduct issue as well!

Another situation that frequently arises is where one party has already left the former matrimonial home, leaving the other in residence and it is agreed that the house has to be sold. Under those circumstances it is often also agreed that the solicitor acting for the resident party shall have the day-to-day conduct of the sale, and of course, from a practical viewpoint, that makes sense, and there is nothing wrong with that *provided the other party is separately represented* – and not just represented in name only, where the other solicitor is merely acting as a post-box. The other party's solicitor should be advising, and attending on, them.

However, even in that situation, the fact is that *because* only one person can carry out the mechanics of the conveyancing, that person is actually acting for both parties in that respect. It means that both husband and wife have to be given costs information, instructions taken from both and the same information given to both. If a solicitor intends not to carry out certain duties for one of the two, he must be very careful when drafting the terms of the retainer with that party.

Very often the reason the same solicitor ends up acting for both parties is for perceived reasons of economy i.e. the saving of one set of legal fees. Don't do it.

The snag is that Sod's Law dictates that if something can go wrong, it will. And don't think it won't happen to you. You will never cease to be amazed at the capacity and ingenuity of parties to a divorce to manufacture grounds for dispute from even the most insignificant of matters. Your problem is – what do you do when, having exchanged contracts, and only a day before completion, some absolutely trivial point suddenly assumes monumental importance to both parties, with one refusing to sign the Transfer, or give possession, until the other concedes?

Under those circumstances, it is very difficult not to treat the client you, or your firm, represented in the divorce more favourably than the other. Indeed, you will probably find your divorce client *expecting* more favourable treatment.

Take the example of a complaint where there had been a very acrimonious divorce. Eventually the court made an order whereby the matrimonial home was to be sold "forthwith" and, because both sides agreed and the wife was still in residence, provided for her solicitors to have conduct of the sale. The husband was, for want of a less polite term, viciously vindictive. Throughout the proceedings he had done his best at all times to spite his wife and cause her as much aggravation as he could. The sale of the house was not important to him – he had moved out and bought himself another property long ago.

The house was put on the market and a buyer found and the wife also found herself a new house. She was dependent on the share of the net proceeds she was to receive to enable her to purchase her new house. The snag was that the purchaser of the matrimonial home was prepared to complete on 24 January but the vendor of the house the wife wanted to buy could not complete until 7 February.

The husband, quoting the word "forthwith" in the Order, and pointing out that it meant "immediately" insisted the sale be completed on 24 January, and so instructed the solicitors. They ignored him and went ahead and completed on 7 February, coinciding the completion with the wife's purchase.

The husband, furious that his plan to have his ex-wife thrown out on the pavement for two weeks had not worked, now turned his wrath on the solicitors and lodged a complaint that they, who, as he pointed out, were acting for him, just as much as for the wife, had ignored his instructions.

Under those circumstances the solicitors really should have refused to continue to act for either party and sent both of them off to other solicitors but they knew that that would certainly have resulted in the sale not even being completed on 7 February and may well have resulted in the loss of the purchaser altogether and to the sale of the house having to start all over again. (It was possible that the ex-husband would have preferred that to have happened, because it would have meant his ex-wife losing the house she wanted, but it would have put him in a bad light to have said so.)

The solicitors were lucky in that the pragmatic view was taken that they had acted in a way that they considered to be in the best interest of both clients under the circumstances and no action was taken against them.

Technically that was possibly not right, but the point is that if you find yourself in such a situation, be on your guard, particularly if there is a history of acrimony between the parties.

Practitioners who are pure conveyancers and who operate in a practice which has a separate divorce section and who are therefore likely to be presented with a situation where they are expected to act for both parties to a divorce in the sale of the former matrimonial home would be well advised to take pre-emptive action to forestall any such situation. They should tell their divorce practitioner colleagues that, if they present them with any such situation, the divorce practitioners will have to do the conveyancing themselves because they were the ones responsible for creating the risk and they can take it.

## 3. Inaccurate cost estimates

This mainly arises by not differentiating between the actual divorce decree and the ancillary matters when asked how much a divorce will cost.

Remember, when asked how much a divorce will cost – whether it has been specifically mentioned or not – to explain that any quote given does not include ancillary matters (remembering to explain what they are!) and is only for obtaining the decree of divorce itself.

Practitioners know that considerations with regard to the divorce decree and anything else are entirely separate issues. Clients do not. When they talk of "divorce" they will usually mean everything connected with it.

## 4. Delay

It is sometimes said that the most stressful thing a person can do is to buy a house. It is not – it is getting divorced. That must be remembered at all times. Because people feel under stress, they want to get what is bothering them over and done with. Because of this they have a tendency to be less tolerant and they start to perceive delay where they usually would not. There is, perhaps, not a lot that the practitioner can do about this except to be aware of the situation and to make sure that, as a result, the client is more than ever kept fully informed about what is going on and the reasons for any period when progress is not being made.

## 5. Lack of information

This arises, for example, where the Decree Absolute is imminent but the client still does not know what is to happen about the house or children.

This is again attributable to the same symptoms as are identified in 4 above and results from an understandable anxiety on the client's part to be kept fully informed about something that assumes the most consuming aspect of their lives.

## 6. A lack of understanding about the statutory charge

This is unforgivable and should have been explained both orally and in writing to the client until the solicitor was absolutely sure the client understood. Notwithstanding, it is clear from continuing complaints about this being received at the CCS, that not every divorce client is getting the relevant information, at least in a way that is understandable to them. Solicitors should not just rely on the hand-outs prepared by the Legal Services Commission, but, as mentioned earlier, should take it upon themselves to explain what the statutory charge is in language the client can understand.

### 7. Not following the client's wishes

This is usually a husband's complaint and arises when solicitors adopt an aggressive attitude in letters, when, in fact, the client wanted the matter to be dealt with in a low-key or conciliatory way (and don't forget, this won't be known unless the client is asked!).

The complaint might arise when the husband suddenly begins to experience difficulties in getting access to his children. The cause of that may not be anything to with the solicitor's approach but the client, who is casting around for something, or someone, to blame, then invariably accuses the solicitor of being responsible because of his wrong approach and the total misman- agement of the whole case.

This is all part and parcel of listening to the client and managing their expec- tations. The mistake arises because of the professional's propensity to presume that he knows best and the client should meekly accept his way of doing things.

Do not forget that the client will know the opponent far better than do you and consequently the client might just have a better idea of the tactics that are most likely to achieve the desired outcome.

### The other side

There is one final area about which complaint is commonly made which is not mentioned in the list above. This is because there is little that a solicitor can actively do to prevent it. This refers to concerns about what is perceived by the client as misconduct by the opponent's solicitor. Most times, of course, it is not, but solicitors can assist their professional colleagues by explaining, should the client mention the matter, that the opponent's solicitors are required to do their best for their client, just as you are for him, and very often this can mean the opponent's solicitor acting in a way that the client may think is wrong, but is not, in fact, improper.

# CONVEYANCING

The main grounds for complaint in conveyancing matters are:

## 1. Inaccurate costs information

This results from:

- revising an estimate where the work turns out to be more onerous than expected, but not telling the client immediately that is known – sometimes not until the bill is rendered;

- charging for abortive work where the client has either not been told that such a charge would be made or the charge itself is out of all proportion to, or even exceeds, the original quotation for the completion of the whole job!

## 2. Errors in completion statements

It is very embarrassing to ask the client for an amount needed to complete a purchase and then to have to contact him in a panic on the morning of completion to ask for more. It is even more embarrassing to account to a client after completion and then either to have to write asking for more money, or, even worse, to have to ask the client for money back that he has been overpaid.

Remember that it is the solicitor's job to get it right, not the client's job to check that the solicitor has got it right. It is part of what a solicitor is paid for. Excuses like 'the client obviously didn't check the statement' or 'the client must have known he was getting more than expected' just won't wash.

The main cause of these kind of errors are:

- failing to read the mortgage instructions, especially where familiarity has bred contempt. Many mortgagees' instructions are not particularly easy to read and it is easy, once they become familiar, to stop reading them properly. Once that habit starts, it is easy to miss the clause saying a retention is going to be made and realisation only dawns when the mortgage advance is received.

- failing to check the information on the client ledger. It is surprising how many times information that is on the ledger when the completion statement is drawn up is missed. Usually the items relates to an unusual search fee, or a survey, that has been forgotten, but essentially the fault lies in not actually checking the information which is on the ledger.

One precaution that can be taken is to ensure that some three or four weeks after completion when all the transactions on the account should have gone through, to revisit the ledger and check that there are nil balances right across both Client and Office account. If that is not the case, it is far easier to sort it out then, while the matter is still reasonably fresh in the mind, rather than to have it brought to your attention months later.

- The making of simple errors such as transposing figures when the statement is drawn up, so that a balance of £3899 carried down from a sale, suddenly becomes a brought forward figure of £8399 for the purchase. This is then compounded if there is a failure to make proper use of the monthly balance, or if the book-keeper fails to alert the responsible partner to any apparent anomalies. Too often the monthly balance is just left to gather dust on the accounts room shelf.

### 3. Outstanding service charges/ground rent

Clients do get very upset if, months after moving into their new home, they are suddenly asked to pay for liabilities that should have been cleared on completion because they were the responsibility of the previous owner.

### 4. The discovery of encumbrances after completion

This might be planning applications with regard to adjoining property, or the discovery of rights of way over the property. The usual cause of this is a failure to insist on getting proper answers to pre-contract enquiries. For example, the answer 'the purchaser should inspect' when the question asks whether something is known to the vendor. Such replies should never be accepted when the seller is the previous owner who has occupied the property.

A word here also about local searches. This is another matter about which the public is becoming aware. Unfortunately awareness is not so great about the limitations on local searches and, it seems, the public imagine that a local search will tell anything that is planned to happen within a radius that far exceeds reality. Advise clients what the limits are. Tell them, if they want any wider information, you can tell them where to go to get it. If they want you to do it, it is going to cost them extra.

### 5. Delay in the registration of title

This is particularly important when the delay only becomes apparent when the client wants to sell.

### 6. The client not knowing exactly what he owns

This frequently arises when clients are asked to sign plans on purchases of new houses that are subject to first registration. The client assumes, probably because he is being asked to sign something, that the solicitor has checked it and is saying that it is accurate. It can arise, however, with regard to any plan that purports to show what the client is buying and which is supplied, directly or indirectly through the solicitor. The prudent practitioner will always tell the client that he is not a surveyor and has not checked the accuracy of any plan produced to the client and that if the client has any doubts as to its accuracy, he should instruct his own surveyor (and put it in writing).

The OSS had a case where the only plan that had ever been supplied to the purchasers was one attached to a mining search, which plan had been prepared by The Coal Authority and which did not accurately show the boundaries of the property. It purported to include within the title the site of a right of way some 25 feet wide and it was only after completion that the right of way came to light. The purchasers had assumed that the plan accurately delineated the boundaries of the land they were buying and that the site of the right of way fell within their title and that they would be able to fence it off. What made matters worse was the fact that they had raised written queries about the possibility of any such encumbrance before exchange of contracts, which the solicitor had ignored.

This complaint also combined elements of head 4 above, because the solicitor had also failed to provide, or show to the complainants, a copy of a conveyance made some ten years earlier to which was attached an accurate plan, not only showing the correct boundaries, clearly excluding the land forming the right of way, but which clearly marked the right of way as such on that plan.

Then, when the matters were raised again after completion, the solicitor compounded matters by seeking to impose further charges for dealing with the very queries the complainants had raised before completion and which the solicitor had ignored.

### 7. Acting in conflict situations

The situation in regard to divorce situations has already been covered, but there is another scenario that also gives rise to problems and it is acting on both sides of a conveyancing matter in a "family" situation.

If a solicitor has an existing client and is then asked to act for relatives of the client on the other side of a conveyancing transaction, there is nothing to prevent him from doing so (Practice Rule 6 (2)), **but** care must be taken, before starting to act, to explain to **both** parties that should a conflict arise between them, they will both be asked to seek separate representation.

# PROBATE

Probate is very much a law unto itself and the scope for complaint appears to be inexhaustible. Often the impulse for complaint is provided by greed on the part of avaricious beneficiaries or from those who thought they ought to have been beneficiaries.

The main areas of complaint on probate matters are, undoubtedly:

- delay in the administration of the estate

- mistakes in the final accounts

- failing to ensure that all creditors are cleared e.g. tax or all legacies paid

Generally speaking, if there is any common ground in the nature of complaints, it is provided by delay in the administration of the estate. One thing that legatees cannot bear is being kept out of their money.

It is surprising how many probate complaints founded on delay are found to be justified. Somewhat similar to divorce complaints, it is almost as if the solicitor, having done all the hard work, perhaps only needing to do the final accounts, then puts the matter to one side, no doubt thinking something like – "Right, it won't take a tick to finish that off" and then getting on with something new, and perhaps by then, more interesting, completely forgetting, not only to actually finish the job off, but also how time is passing.

When a file is put to one side of the desk, waiting for that spare two or three hours that are necessary to finish the job off, remember that those two or three hours are never likely to occur, and that the longer the file stays there, the more it becomes part of the desk until the fee-earner eventually stops noticing it at all. What then makes matters worse is when the beneficiaries enquire of the solicitor what is causing the delay and get no response.

The following case is not at all untypical of probate complaints that reach the CCS and combined almost all of the above features.

It came from a man who was one of five residuary beneficiaries, the other four all being charities. The estate itself was, on the face of it, relatively simple, consisting of a house, three Halifax Building Society accounts and one or two other minor assets.

The deceased died in June 1995. Probate was obtained in November 1995 and the sale of the house was completed in March 1996. Ostensibly, the estate could now be distributed, but the fly in the ointment was that the Halifax Building Society was about to convert and make a bonus share issue. The beneficiaries could not agree on what to do. The charities wanted the money due to them. The complainant wanted to keep the money in the accounts in order to benefit from the share issue.

Eventually it was agreed that sufficient would be retained in the accounts to enable the complainant to obtain the share issue and the rest would be distributed between the charities and that the individual would be solely entitled to all the shares eventually received.

The relevant part of the estate was then distributed between the charities in April 1996. So far, so good. However, by the time the remainder of the estate came to be finalised, in November 1997, the solicitors appeared to have not only forgotten what had previously happened, but also somehow managed to over-calculated the payments due to the charities by some £6000, leaving the complainant short by that sum.

Then, in January 1999, when the problem had still not been resolved and the complainant was beginning to lose patience and referred the matter to the OSS, the firm suddenly queried the complainant's right to the whole of the share issue.

The matter was not ultimately resolved until July 2000. In the meantime, the firm had also failed to reply to no fewer than 25 communications between March 1998 and July 1999.

Here, then, is a firm who did all the initial work perfectly well up to the time when the estate could be distributed. After then, however, there was a catalogue of delay, confusion and mistakes, all compounded by the firm completely ignoring the complainant. As the complainant was not actually the client, all the OSS could do was to reduce the firm's costs by £1000, about 20% of their total profit costs.

As stated, the complainant in the case quoted was not the client of the solicitors concerned and there was a consequent restriction on OSS powers.

## Who is the client?

A question that seems to vex probate practitioners more than any other relates to a solicitor's responsibilities under Rule 15 and to whom those responsibilities are owed. The question is who should the practitioner regard as his client in probate matters and what, if any, duties does he owe to those who are not his clients? To answer this it is necessary to begin with some basic points.

Firstly, in dealing with an estate, the only person who can be the solicitor's client is the executor, or, obviously, the executors if there are more than one.

It follows that the executor is the only person to whom a solicitor owes a duty under Rule 15 and so is the only person to whom costs information needs to be given and, subject to the exception mentioned below, is the only person who can raise a service complaint that the solicitor is obliged to deal with.

Secondly, only a client can benefit from a compensatory award in the event of a finding of inadequate professional service (IPS) by the CCS, so that a compensatory award can only be made in favour of an executor.

Thirdly, the CCS does not need a complaint from a client to enable it to investigate complaints of IPS. Any doubts about this were removed by Schedule 7 para 11(2)(c) of the Access to Justice Act 1999.

Having said that, the CCS will not normally accept complaints of inadequate service from someone who is not a client of the solicitor complained of. The reason is that solicitors only owe a duty of service to their own clients. Usually, when complaints come from another source, they either come from the other party in a matter i.e. the opponent whose interests are diametrically opposed to those of the solicitor's own client, or from interfering relatives who do not like the result achieved, even though the client may be quite content.

However, that situation does not hold good in probate matters and it does not take much thought to realise why. As will be readily appreciated, it would be nonsensical to have a situation where beneficiaries, who are not clients of the solicitor because he himself is the executor and is therefore his own client, had to refer complaints to the solicitor because he was the executor, and, as executor, he could then just tell the beneficiaries that they had no grounds for complaint and he was satisfied that he, with his solicitor's hat on, was dealing with things perfectly properly.

If residuary beneficiaries, who are more interested than anyone else in the adequate handling of the estate, were not able raise genuine complaints with the CCS, they would have no redress and no-one they could turn to for help if, for instance, there was unreasonable delay in the winding up of the estate, without having to embark on potentially expensive litigation.

If such complaints are found to be substantiated, the only sanction available is a reduction in the solicitor's fees, with, obviously, a consequent increase in the size of the residuary estate that would benefit the residuary beneficiaries.

Applying the above principles, it would now be appropriate to examine the three scenarios that can arise.

1.  Where the executors of a will are laymen and have no connection with the solicitor's firm and the solicitor is instructed by the executors to obtain probate and to act in the administration of the estate.
    Here, the situation is clear. It is the executor (or both of them if there is more than one) who is the client and it is the executor to whom all the information required by Practice Rule 15 should be given and he is the only person entitled to make a complaint with which the solicitor is expected to deal in accordance with his firm's Complaints Procedure.
    That, however, is not very "consumer-friendly" as far as the Residuary Beneficiary is concerned – and he is the one who is, in reality, paying the bill. In such cases practitioners should be encouraged to ask the executors

if they have any thing against the solicitor supplying the residuary beneficiary with costs information and keeping them in touch with developments. If they haven't, then it can be done.

If a complaint is received from a residuary beneficiary, do not just send them away with the excuse that they are not the client. Instead explain that the complaint cannot be addressed without the consent of the client – i.e. the executor(s) – but if they are happy for the practitioner to deal with the residuary beneficiary's concerns, it will be done. Also remember that this only applies to residuary beneficiaries, not any old legatee.

In practice it is found that many complaints arise out of disagreements between beneficiaries and executors. If a complaint is received from a beneficiary, whether specific or residuary, there is no compulsion on a solicitor to deal with it and the beneficiary can be politely referred to the executor with an accompanying explanation that it is the executor who is the client and that it would, therefore not be correct for you, the solicitor, to correspond with the beneficiary, because it would involve a breach of the duty of confidentiality to the client.

2.    Where the solicitor, or a member of his firm, is appointed to be the executor of the will and he so acts in obtaining probate and administering the estate. (The following observations will, of course, apply equally to cases where there is more than one executor and all the executors are members of the same firm.)

In those circumstances the solicitor/executor is his own client and there is no *obligation* upon the solicitor to give costs, or any other Rule 15, information to anyone else and the solicitor will not suffer a costs reduction or be required by the OSS to pay compensation for failing, for example, to give costs information to a residuary beneficiary, but the same comments as before are equally applicable.

With regard to the question of general service complaints e.g. delay, failing to account etc. the position, as indicated above, is somewhat different.

It is to guard against that kind of situation, where, in effect, a solicitor can act as judge in his own cause, that the CCS *will* contemplate complaints by a residuary beneficiary where there is no lay executor who can take up the complaints on behalf of the residuary beneficiaries. The solicitor will also be expected to deal with them as if the residuary beneficiary were the client.

3.    Where the solicitor is a joint executor with a layman. Here the situation is more complicated and less definite.

All really depends on the nature, or standing, of the lay executor. This is where it all becomes something less than an exact science, as one has to make a judgement about the standing of the lay executor.

In these circumstances, as will now be readily appreciated, it is the solicitor and the lay executor together who are the clients. The lay executor is the person who is entitled to the Rule 15 information and from whom the solicitor has to accept complaints.

If the lay co-executor is not even a beneficiary of any kind and has been appointed simply because he was an old friend of the deceased and someone the deceased felt could be relied upon to see that his wishes were carried out, his function with regard to the realisation of the estate being restricted to signing forms, he may well not have sufficient personal interest to pursue any complaint raised by a beneficiary. Under those circumstances, particularly if the lay executor is elderly, the situation would not be regarded in the same way.

It is still the lay executor who is the solicitor's client and who is the person solely entitled to the relevant information under Rule 15. There would still be no redress for a residuary beneficiary who received no costs information, but he could get redress, albeit indirectly by way of a costs reduction, for other complaints related to the service afforded.

The position is different with regard to dealing with complaints, because it is more akin to that under 2 above, and, consequently, the OSS would expect a solicitor to deal with complaints that come from any one, or more, of the residuary beneficiaries.

The difficulty, of course, is that the position may not be quite so clear cut as it is in the examples given above so that one would be forced into making a subjective decision as to whether or not complaints ought to be dealt with under the firm's Complaints Procedure.

Perhaps the better common sense *and* commercial view would be, and it is an attitude that the CCS would encourage, that no matter what the strict interpretation may be, it would be in the interests of good client relations to treat all residuary beneficiaries as if they were clients, even if, strictly speaking, they are not. Certainly, the CCS would prefer solicitors to deal with service complaints from residuary beneficiaries as if they were clients. That would also seem to be the view taken by the Ombudsman and consumer organisations who, it would appear, would like to see a harder line taken whereby solicitors were obliged to accept and deal with complaints from residuary beneficiaries.

On 4 March 2004 the Law Society announced it would consider complaints from "a wider range of beneficiaries". However, it appears that the same restriction on CCS powers as outlined above still apply and all that the CCS will try to do is obtain explanations etc for the complaining beneficiary while making it clear to the "complainant" that the complaint cannot be the subject of an inadequacy of service investigation.

However, it is possible to conceive of circumstances where that may not be desirable, for example if the complaint arises from a family squabble, or if just one of many residuary beneficiaries seeks to raise a matter when all the others are perfectly happy. There was, for instance, one complaint referred to the OSS by a residuary beneficiary who refused to sign the accounts until his complaints had been dealt with to his satisfaction, thus holding up the distribution of the estate to each of the other 22 residuary beneficiaries, all of whom had no complaint whatsoever.

It is also fair to say that, subject to how many of them there are, the OSS would like solicitor/executors to give Rule 15 information to residuary beneficiaries and keep them informed of progress, although there is no obligation to do so. Indeed, it may be thought sensible, from both a public relations and a "potential client" point of view, to do this, thus treating such people at all times as if they are clients.

Perhaps the best way of addressing that type of situation, assuming the practitioner is prepared to do so, would be to write to the residuary beneficiaries at the outset of the matter giving them the normal costs information and explaining that, although it is the executor who is the client, the practitioner is prepared, if the residuary beneficiaries *all* agree, to keep them informed as to progress at set intervals and also setting out the anticipated cost of giving them that information, or explaining how the cost will be calculated. It can be explained that it is necessary for them all to agree in order to avoid a complaint from any beneficiary who later maintains they did not want such information and that costs have been wasted.

It should also be born in mind that, in cases where there is no lay executor, residuary beneficiaries have the specific right to apply for a Remuneration Certificate.

# CRIMINAL

Here the solicitor is on a hiding to nothing. It is a fact that there are many criminals who are convinced, or convince themselves, they are innocent, or at least that they should not have been convicted, and are only in prison due to, one, or a combination of bent police, corrupt judges or incompetent lawyers.

The biggest danger here is failing to keep the client informed, that is to say, not telling the client the reasons for taking a particular line of action. The CCS will not question a solicitor's exercise of his professional judgement. Every criminal lawyer is frequently called upon to make decisions about how a case should be run, whether to opt for a Crown Court hearing, whether the client should make a statement etc. In making such decisions each solicitor will use his professional judgement and that judgement may differ from one person to another. It is partly that which makes one lawyer better than another. That does not mean, however, that the standards of service should be any different. But of course, what has just been referred to, does not relate to service. The CCS is not empowered to judge a solicitor's competence, only his standards of service.

However, beware the situation where you judge it to be dangerous or inadvisable to follow the client's instructions or wishes.

This most frequently arises when the client wants you to call certain witnesses in his defence, but you know that at best they will be unhelpful and at worst will guarantee the client's conviction if they are called. The inevitable result, when they are not called and the client is convicted anyway, is that he is convinced that the only reason that he was convicted is because of the failure to call the witnesses.

That is not to say that the solicitor has to blindly follow what the client says he wants to be done, regardless of his own better judgement – there would certainly be conduct proceedings awaiting if some of the more bizarre requests were complied with. It is, however, essential that the solicitor covers his own flank by explaining to the client, both verbally and confirming it in writing, why he is not prepared to follow the client's wishes. That is what is meant by failing to keep the client informed. A situation may, of course, arise where, if the client is not prepared to accept what he is advised, that the solicitor can no longer represent the client. That, however, does not absolve him from the duty to explain his reasoning to the client. Failure to keep the client properly informed is the biggest single ground upon which successful complaints in criminal matters are founded.

The other, which large criminal practices who tend to departmentalise their activities should be aware of, arises from that very departmentalisation, where one person will take instructions, another will do the court appearances (and possibly several different persons will be involved in that alone) another will see the client on remand, another will do the brief and yet another appear behind counsel.

Again, how a practice chooses to organise its work is its own affair, but practitioners should be aware that it can, and does, give rise to allegations that, because the personnel kept changing, no-one knew what was going on etc and the client is only the more convinced about that if he keeps getting asked the same questions or to provide the same information.

This is not necessarily a ground of complaint that is going to be found to be substantiated, but, provided practitioners are aware of dangers, the necessary action can be taken to avoid complaints of that nature and so avoid both the complaint and the subsequent wasted time that will have to be spent in dealing with it.

# PART TWO:
# DEALING WITH COMPLAINTS

# CHAPTER FOUR
# WHAT'S THE PROBLEM?

This part of this book should really be sub-titled "The Myth, the Motive, the Method" – and with good reason.

Before anyone can hope to start to deal with complaints in a way that is acceptable to the client, it is necessary that they have the correct mental approach, which essentially means approaching complaints in a positive frame of mind rather than a negative one, which entails that inward groan and the thought "Oh, no, Well, let's get it over and done with."

That kind of attitude does tend to come naturally in any event, because no-one really likes to accept criticism, which is what dealing with complaints essentially means. Unfortunately there are several factors which contribute in no small measure to that attitude amongst lawyers.

These are the myths, to which I have referred above and it is firstly necessary to dispel those myths. As long as those beliefs are held, the right approach to complaints handling will not be adopted and followed.

The next step is to demonstrate that there are good reasons why firms should adopt a policy whereby, even if the partners do not actually encourage complaints, they certainly do not discourage them and deal with them properly when they do arise. There are seven such reasons.

If it is accepted that the myths are exactly that, and that there are good, logical reasons why complaints should be approached in a positive frame of mind, there is a good chance that the correct methods of dealing with them will be employed to good effect.

One common belief that prevails, which is not included in the list of myths which follow, but which could well have done, is that the legal profession is, in some way, being singled out for special attention as far as complaints are concerned; that people are being specifically encouraged to raise complaints about their solicitors. That just is not so. You only have to take a look at the medical profession to know that. The fact is that, these days, no-one is exempt from client, or customer, expectations and the resultant complaints when those expectations are not met. In fact, managing expectations is one of the greatest failings in the legal profession, but, for more about that, see page 4 on Complaints Avoidance.

However, take any walk of life, teachers, banks, the motor, or railway industries, plumbers, you name it – they all get their fair share of complaints.

There could not have been a profession whose members, generally speaking showed more arrogance towards its "customers" than the medical profession – not even lawyers – but doctors have recognised the fact and are doing something about it. Gone is the phrase "Doctor knows best." These days the GMC are actually training doctors, by means of courses which doctors are required to attend, on how to develop a proper relationship with their patients, something which there is no sign of the Law Society even contemplating at the present time.

It is an unfortunate fact that most solicitors seem to find it difficult to deal, in an acceptable way, with complaints. The problem is that most solicitors do not seem to agree, but every independent Consumer Organisation in the country tells them that it is so; so does their Regulatory body and so does the Legal Services Ombudsman.

Consider these extracts from the 1999 Annual Report published by the Legal Services Ombudsman.

> "The ever increasing volumes of complaints (being received) at the OSS are symptoms of the problem, not the problem itself."

> "Solicitors themselves need to shoulder the responsibility of client care and accept that effective complaints handling by the firm is an integral part of it."

> "Solicitors' failure to embrace the concept of client care; defensiveness and refusal to admit mistakes lead(s) to escalation of client dissatisfaction."

Research also confirms that a high proportion of solicitors think they are good at handling complaints. Unfortunately a higher proportion of complainants and complaint handlers at both the CCS and the LSO's office think otherwise.

There is a distinct and deep gulf in perception about this between the profession and just about everyone else, but the problem for the profession is how to improve complaint handling techniques so that solicitors get it right. One thing is for sure, if the complaint is not handled in an acceptable way, it does not matter how much in the right the solicitor may be, the client is just going to become more and more disaffected and more and more insistent.

This gulf between the perceptions of complaints handlers and the profession was vividly illustrated by a Report by the Customer Management Consultancy Ltd for the LSO's Office and published in May 1999. Bear in mind that this Survey was carried out with reference to complaints that had been referred to the LSO's office and had therefore been through the OSS procedures. The survey sought the views of both the solicitors who were the subject of the complaints and the complaint handlers who had dealt with it. The results were quite startling.

They showed that while half the solicitors surveyed thought they had handled the complaints well, virtually all complaint handlers thought the complaints could have been dealt with much better than they had been.

9 out of 10 solicitors thought their standards of service were high, while 7 out of 10 complaint handlers thought their standards of service could have been significantly improved.

Half the solicitors thought that complaints were seldom, if ever, justified, while complaint handlers said that virtually always *some part* of *every* complaint was justified.

What is the truth, and what has caused this huge difference in perception between the regulators and the regulated and what can be done about it?

The first step is to be honest with oneself. Whether lawyers like it or not, the fact is that most of them are awful at handling complaints. This, then, might be a good place to summarise what it is about lawyers that makes them so bad at it. What follows is a list of those characteristics commonly found in lawyers and which contribute to that situation. If anyone is possessed of any one of them, then handling complaints in an acceptable way is made difficult – and the more that one possesses, the more difficult it is. All of the characteristics listed will be found cropping up time and again in the pages that follow and some of them will be dealt with in more detail.

To summarise, then, they are:

- The belief that they know best about everything and clients should just accept what they say and do without question

- The confusion of issues of negligence with issues of service

- Regarding complaints as a personal affront or a slur on the firm

- The confusion of technical excellence and ability with matters of service

- Holding on to the myths about the type of person who complains

- Not believing there are good reasons for dealing with complaints properly

- Taking complaints at face value

- Not accepting that what they *really* need to do is to accept they have an unhappy client and to find out why

If all that is then taken against the background that solicitors have been trained to react to situations defensively or confrontationally, the wonder is that there are *any* solicitors who deal appropriately with complaints!

# CHAPTER FIVE
# COMPLAINTS PROCEDURES

One thing that it is essential that every firm should have in place is a proper complaints procedure. This is essential because, not only do the Rules of Conduct governing the profession say that every firm must have in place a written complaints procedure, but it gives a framework within which a complaint can be tackled with the best chance of achieving a satisfactory result for all concerned. Furthermore, if a complaint reaches the CCS the firm will be expected to demonstrate how they have dealt with it in accordance with their procedure. If they have no written procedure in place this is impossible to do.

It is apparent that a considerable number of firms either still do not have a written complaints procedure or fondly imagine they have, when, in fact, what they have is unsatisfactory.

A common belief among sole practitioners, or small firms, is that they do not need a written procedure because it is obvious who is going to deal with the complaint. Well, that is not necessarily so. There are many sole practitioners who, to give the client more reassurance, have entered into arrangements with other sole practitioners to act as each others complaint handlers, and, provided the client agrees (remember the confidentiality issue) there is a lot to be said for this.

Another plus is that the complainant can be given a copy of the procedure. Indeed, solicitors are required to do this if the client asks for a copy. Again, if there is nothing in writing, this is an impossibility.

Every procedure should give the client certain information. They want to know WHO is going to deal with my complaint; WHAT are they going to do, in practical terms, and WHEN will it all be done.

In the Appendix the reader will find specimen complaint procedures for all sizes of firm. Remember, they are precedents. They give possible courses of action, all of which may not be available to every practitioner. So, if a particular alternative is not available, omit it. It is possible that a complaint will arise from not meeting clients' expectations. It is unforgiveable if the sin should be repeated when handling the consequent complaint.

Some firms have taken their "procedure" from publications that are now outdated. This applies to the procedures contained in "Keeping Clients" published in 1997 and an even older publication, "Client Care – a Guide for Solicitors." Generally speaking if a firm's procedure has not been revised since the new millennium, it is obsolete and should be revised.

An observation about Complaint Resolution Forms. These do not necessarily come from the CCS – they can be obtained from other sources. Even if supplied by the CCS to the client, the CCS has nothing on record about the complaint. They do not, therefore, have to have the response to the complaint copied to them. The whole purpose of a Complaint Resolution Form is to afford the solicitor the opportunity of resolving the complaint *without* the CCS becoming involved.

# CHAPTER SIX
# WHY BOTHER?
# DESTROYING THE MYTHS

## THE OBJECTIONS

Talk to almost any solicitor about complaints and it can be anticipated that there will often be one or more of three reactions.

They are that complaints are:

1. only made to try and avoid payment of the bill

2. only made by crackpots

3. 'nearly always unjustified and, anyway, I know perfectly well how to deal with complaints.' In fact, the first part of that statement positively disproves the accuracy of the second.

### Bill avoiders?

Of course, there are people who make complaints solely to try to avoid paying their bill. But, in fact, they form a small proportion of complainants. The suggestion that is consistently made by those who hold to that view, is that the only way to satisfy a complainant is to give in and make some monetary concession. This particularly rankles when there is a suspicion that the client is a professional complainer who never intended to pay his bill in the first place.

There are such people about and the only way to tackle them is to try to ensure that no client has any grounds upon which to make a justifiable complaint about the service he has received. But, as regards the genuine complainant, it is always possible to deal with the complaint in such a way that, even if the complaint is considered to be unjustified, the client at least thinks he has been listened to and that the solicitor, has not been defensive, aggressive, patronising, argumentative and all the other adjectives commonly used to describe the way that solicitors address complaints.

The misconception that complaints are only made to try and avoid payment of the bill commonly arises when a complaint is not made until a bill is rendered and this then colours the way that the matter is approached with the solicitor invariably tending to adopt a dismissive attitude.

There can, in fact be other, very good, reasons why a client does not complain during the time his case is still live. In 1997, the University of the West of England published their findings from research they carried out which revealed that one of the reasons why clients did not complain until *after* the job had been finished was because of their fear that if they complained while it was still ongoing, it would have an adverse effect on the way the solicitor dealt with the matter thereafter and would upset to an even greater degree, what, in all probability, was an already deteriorating solicitor/client relationship.

If complainants are asked why, if matters are as bad as they say, do they not think they ought to consider changing to another solicitor, a common response is "No, I think I'd better just keep quiet for the moment. If I do anything now it will just make matters worse."

In fact, the same research revealed that only a minority of complainants were looking for financial compensation when they made their complaints. The majority were more concerned with being listened to and having their concerns acknowledged and receiving reassurance and information.

Witness a complaint that came to the OSS which had got totally out of hand and illustrates, not only the false assumption that the client was after money, but also the misconception about the nature of complaints and the gulf that exists between the profession and the public in this respect.

The client had written to the solicitors expressing concern about delays in a conveyancing matter. She ended her letter "As senior partner I respectfully ask what you are prepared to do about the situation. I conclude by asking for an appointment to see you." Here is a client expressing concern about the service she is receiving and wanting to see the senior partner with a view to resolving matters.

Her letter prompted the following reply:

> "I consider it appropriate that I deal with the points raised in correspondence rather than meet you to go through these points and I will respond in the very near future. Your penultimate paragraph asks what we are prepared to do about the situation. I would ask you to clarify if it is monetary compensation that you seek. If so, I must assume from this that you consider that this firm has been professionally negligent and it would be inappropriate for me to comment on such matters other than to address the point that you have raised."

That reply betrayed several common mistakes.

1. The solicitor wanted to deal with the complaint on his terms, rather than the client's, i.e. in writing, rather than have a meeting when the latter is far preferable and stands a much better chance of achieving a successful resolution of the matter.

2. The solicitor jumped to a conclusion, with no evidence, that the client wanted financial compensation, and then to compound matters:

3. He confused issues of negligence with issues of inadequacy of service.

How he could have even thought that the complaint amounted to negligence, or even that the client was making such an allegation is incomprehensible. Under those circumstances, perhaps the client's response was hardly surprising.

> "I look forward to your response to the points I raised. I am not seeking monetary compensation. The thought never crossed my mind, but I did think, after you had received my letter, that an apology would have been made...Had that been promptly made, the matter would have rested there. I can only conclude by saying that I am very disappointed with the service that I have received from your office."

In fact a too quick offer of financial compensation often produces the reaction amongst complainants that they are being fobbed off and convinces them that their complaint is the tip of the iceberg and that the solicitor has something to hide!

## Crackpots?

It is also true that there are complaints which are made by crackpots, but they, also, form a very small proportion of those received by the CCS. And even crackpots cannot be entirely ignored – they too have friends and relatives who will listen to them.

## Unjustified?

But it is the third misconception that is, perhaps, the most invidious. This commonly arises when a client makes a complaint that comprises several issues. CCS caseworkers, who are obliged to look into every complaint thoroughly, will tell you that although a multi-headed complaint may be unjustified in the main, usually, at the heart of every one, there is at least one justified complaint.

What has happened is that the client has started off with one grumble. That has remained undetected and therefore unresolved. That grumble has then festered and multiplied because, with his growing dissatisfaction the client begins to cast around and find other aspects to grumble about until these too multiply, in the client's own mind, into fully grown complaints.

It is these add-ons that are likely to be unjustified, but, when the whole is presented to the solicitor, he perceives that many of the complaints are unjustified and then treats every issue as being unjustified.

It is absolutely essential that what the client is saying is never dismissed as rubbish. The important thing is **not** what the solicitor thinks, but what the client thinks of **him**, no matter how misguided the solicitor thinks he may be.

There are also numerous solicitors who make all the right noises about complaints and complaints handling and who can recite all the rhetoric as well as anyone and who will give assurances that those are the principles that they follow when they have to deal with a complaint. However, the evidence suggests that all their fine words fly out of the window the moment they get a complaint about their own service, and all manner of reasons are found to treat themselves as an exception.

Well, no-one is an exception. What follows applies to **everyone**. One of the first essentials to successful complaint handling is being honest with oneself.

The final misconception is not to do with the nature of complaints, and, for that reason, was not included in the earlier list. It is to do with what can be done about them.

### Communicating with the complainant

Where a complaint has been made that has reached the CCS and in which that Office is involved as a result, that does not preclude a solicitor from communicating directly with the client, or ex-client, about the matter, particularly if it is done in an attempt to resolve the complaint.

Similarly, there is nothing wrong with a solicitor communicating direct to an ex-client *about the complaint,* even when the former client has instructed other solicitors to take over the conduct of the matter, the handling of which has given rise to the complaint. The original retainer must be taken to extend to the handling of any complaint that may arise from that retainer.

It may be a courtesy, of course, to write to the client's new solicitors and tell them what is happening and to ask if they wish to be copied in to any correspondence provided the client gives authority for that to be done, but no-one at the CCS will suggest that it is misconduct to write to an ex-client about complaints they have raised, even when they have instructed other solicitors.

# THE REASONS

Why bother is a question frequently asked by busy practitioners who feel:

- they have far better things to do than to try to mollify disaffected clients who will probably go elsewhere anyway

- it all costs time and money, both of which will be a complete waste if the complaint turns out to be unjustified, which most of them are anyway, and

- it prevents fee-earning work being done and makes it harder to meet targets etc

Suffice it to say that today's client is many times more sophisticated than his counterpart even 10 years ago and simply will not put up with being fobbed off. The profession must accept that times are changing and that, with the active encouragement of the media, this is a complainers' society, particularly where the legal profession is concerned, the public having now been brain-washed into believing that all lawyers are fat-cats who rake in a lot of money for doing very little.

However, let us examine the wider implications.

## Bad publicity

Perhaps the chief motive for dealing with complaints properly is the risk of unwelcome publicity. This can take many forms – disaffected clients can be quite inventive when it comes to taking vengeance on those they perceive to have wronged them. Vengeance can range from actual physical violence – with the consequent publicity – to other public manifestations of dissatisfaction.

One unhappy client in a Midlands town, one night, put up posters on every town centre lamp post, telegraph pole and any other available spot, identi-fying the firm and advising the public not to have anything to do with them if they wanted legal work doing satisfactorily.

## Escalation

The second good reason is the potential for the escalation of the complaint itself. As already indicated, the greater proportion of complaints reaching the CCS are found to be substantiated *to some degree*. Experience shows that many clients start off with one genuine and valid concern. However, when it is not addressed (and, even worse, maybe not even recognised) and is allowed to fester, they convince themselves that there are all manner of additional matters that are grounds for complaint, even if they are not, and would not have become so had the original complaint been dealt with properly. This, incidentally, is a common feature when complaints are stored up and produced after the bill has been rendered.

Such complainants then also begin to attribute to the person acting for them all manner of sinister motives. Every written word is examined pedantically for any small fault or adverse interpretation. The solicitor quickly becomes exasperated at what he sees as an awkward client. The whole thing eventually explodes in a welter of accusation and recrimination which is then characterised by a stubborn refusal on the part of the complainant to believe anything that anyone tells him that runs counter to the situation that he has convinced himself is the case.

By allowing perhaps one minor matter that would have been simple to detect and then resolve at the outset to go unresolved, the solicitor finds that, in the end, he has a whole more complicated and time consuming situation to deal with.

## Market research

One positive benefit to any firm of having a proper complaints handling system is that it can be used as a method of supplying useful information about the practice. It is, in effect, free market research and can tell the partners a lot about how their firm is perceived and what are its weaknesses.

Once that information is available, action can be taken to overcome any shortcomings. One thing that must never be done, however, is to dismiss as rubbish what the client is saying.

Remember, as pointed out earlier, the important thing is **not** what you, the solicitor thinks, but **is** what the client thinks of you. The blunt truth is that the client is telling the firm where they think it is not good enough, and, if several people tell the firm the same thing, there is a definite problem!

It must also constantly be born in mind that, unless the firm is unusual, it will rely on repeat business and recommendations. For that reason any practice simply cannot afford to have a dissatisfied client. It is those firms who actually exceed their client's expectations who will get the recommendations and who will succeed.

Everybody has heard of the, possibly apocryphal, research that one satisfied client will tell five others about the firm, while one dissatisfied client tells twenty three others. However there is research that revealed that only 5% of dissatisfied clients actually raised a complaint with the firm. Assuming the accuracy of the first piece of research, what that means is that for every person dissatisfied with your firm that you know about, a potential 437 people are being told your firm is very poor.

Conversely there is also research which reveals that a dissatisfied client who has had a complaint properly addressed is highly likely to use the firm again and to recommend it to others. However, even if this does not happen, it is worth finding out what went wrong.

Even if the solicitor genuinely feels that the complaint is totally misconceived, he should still be aware that, even if he is right, he still has an unhappy client on his hands. Something, somewhere, has gone wrong and he needs to find out what it is. If he has one client for whom things have gone wrong, he probably has others who are just not telling him about it, but are going round telling anyone who will listen to them to steer clear of him.

## Saving fee-earning time

Also bear in mind how much more fee-earning time might be lost if the complaints find their way to the CCS and time has then to be spent dealing with them. If the solicitor has dealt with the complaint properly, all the work will already have been done and it will only be necessary to copy the relevant documents and send them off, with an account of what was done to try to resolve the matter.

## Professional obligations

In addition to the reasons already set out, there are professional obligations to consider under Practice Rule 15.

The new Rule came into force on 3 September 1999. At this stage it will suffice to point up the relevant aspects which relate to the desirability of handling complaints properly.

The fact is that up to mid-1999 too many firms regarded compliance with the old Rule 15 as something akin to an optional extra. That will no longer wash. The CCS is taking the view that the profession has had warnings and encouragement enough. If there is evidence of a consistent failure to deal with complaints properly in-house, disciplinary proceedings will inevitably follow.

Ultimately, all that is being asked of the profession is that it exhibits the same level of customer care that it, or its members individually, as customers, themselves expect from their own accountant or doctor or, for that matter, from anyone else rendering them a service for which they expect to be paid.

In addition, there is now the prospect of having a costs order made against the firm irrespective of any costs reduction or compensation order that might result. One word about costs orders – they are not automatic, they are discretionary. If the CCS Adjudicator who makes the decision about the complaint can see that irrespective of justification or otherwise, the firm has made a genuine attempt to resolve the matter in-house, the costs order will not follow.

## The OFT

The next good reason is one that is not widely appreciated, and that is the very real possibility of falling foul of the Office for Fair Trading.

Every solicitors' firm is licensed through the Law Society to undertake credit related work under the Consumer Credit Act 1974. That means that the Law Society, through the CCS has to monitor breaches of the Act and act on them. Breaches include unfair business practices, which, in turn, include failing to reply to correspondence from clients and failing to deal properly with client complaints.

Many firms may retort that they don't really care. All the OFT can do is to revoke their license which, in effect, only prevents them from doing debt collection work or arranging mortgages.

But it goes further than that. Not only is there the risk of adverse publicity – because the revocation of licenses is publicised – but there is also the knock-on possibility of the Trading Standards authority becoming involved. And do not think it cannot happen. More than one prosecution has been brought against solicitors' firms for, in effect, failing to comply with their professional obligations under Rule 15!

## Loss of self-regulation

And, finally, the profession may lose self-regulation, although there are those who think that would be no bad thing. However, if that happens, the profession can, in all probability, look forward to even greater financial demands being made on it on an annual basis. A Legal Service Complaints Commissioner (with the LSO doubling up in that role) has already been appointed at some considerable expense (see *Law Society Gazette* 29/4/04) to which the Law Society – and therefore every practitioner – has to contribute. The next step would appear to be that the government will appoint a Regulator who will dictate how complaints will be dealt with and within what timescale, with penalties if those targets are not met. And, of course, it will be the profession who will end up paying any penalty, just as it will have to pay for the cost of the Regulator and any staff he may employ. What is more, if a new Regulator is set up wholly independent of the profession, solicitors can bet double or quits on their overdrafts that the policy will then be a direction to the regulator, "if you can't cope with the staff you've got, then take on more and recoup the cost from the profession, after all, they're the ones who are causing the problem."

# CHAPTER SEVEN
# THE MENTAL APPROACH
# TO COMPLAINTS

Why are solicitors constantly criticised about the way in which they handle complaints?

They are criticised by the LSO, the LCD and just about every Consumer Organisation there is. They all express surprise, horror and disbelief at the way in which solicitors, in general, deal with complaints.

However, it should be no surprise at all that solicitors approach complaints in an entirely unacceptable way. It would be amazing if they did otherwise. Why?

Well, to begin with lawyers have never had any training whatsoever in how to deal with complaints.

Commercial organisations have simple complaints to deal with. Dealing with complaints about shoddy goods is an entirely different proposition to dealing with complaints about service. Even those that deal with what are essentially service issues are mainly simple matters to deal with e.g. my train was late. Those organisations employ specially trained departments to deal with complaints – and even then, some of them still get it wrong!

What chance has the lawyer got when, not only are Complaints about legal services much more complicated, but the lawyer has had no training at all in how to deal with them. Not only that, but a lawyer's day to day work over the years is almost calculated to ensure that he adopts totally the wrong approach to complaints anyway

Why? Because he is representing his client and fighting his corner to the best of his ability. On the other side is another lawyer doing exactly the same. It means that solicitors automatically adopt a defensive or confrontational approach to any situation they are presented with. That approach is instilled in them. They are conditioned by their work to be confrontational and defensive.

The only possible exception is Probate, but it extends even to Conveyancing where the lawyer is still looking after their client's best interests. It is even worse if he is a contentious lawyer. Just think what the word means!

This feature has been remarked on by others, but without relating it to the context of complaint handling. A former local Law Society secretary wrote in an article for a legal journal "...there can be no other profession whose members are individually in opposition to each other on a daily basis. Even soldiers fight together. Whether a client's problems are contentious or non-contentious, a solicitor faces obstruction to what he or she is trying to achieve for a client from a professional "colleague", who is looking after his own client's interests...Every day brings fresh arguments and new opponents... Every legal argument is a battle of wills." His article was about stress, but the observations are no less valid when related to complaints.

Lawyers, by nature are suspicious, pedantic and critical and argumentative. Generally speaking, they are only too willing to argue the toss about anything with anybody at the drop of a hat. They are adept at splitting the finest of hairs and are obsessive about detail to the point of perversity. That may be fine for the purpose of doing one's work – but not for dealing with complaints. If a single trace of any of those characteristics is exhibited in response to a complaint, you are dead in the water before you start.

The trouble is that when a solicitor gets a complaint, that is the way in which he reacts. It's automatic. It's done without thinking or realising that's what is happening or even intending to react that way.

If I sat behind a lawyer dealing with a complaint and, when he had finished, assuming it to be the case, asked him why he had dealt with it so confrontationally, I know what he'd say – "but I wasn't being confrontational, I was just behaving normally!" Yes, he was – he was being confrontational!

When lawyers respond to a complaint in writing they tend to send legalistic responses. They write a letter as if they are writing to another solicitor on the other side of a transaction. The result is that the letter comes across in the same confrontational way.

Too often the CCS comes across responses to complaints that seek to take issue with the words the client has used, or which seek to dissect the matter and take issue with each individual item, instead of accepting that the client is unhappy and trying to find out why.

A former President of the Law Society was once heard to tell a roomful of lawyers "If the client can't express his complaint in a way that you can understand, why waste your time dealing with it?" The answer, of course, is that you still have a client who has a complaint, only now he is more determined than ever to do something about it.

Add to that a natural aversion to criticism – who likes to be criticised? And isn't that effectively what a complaint is? Many seem to treat a complaint as a personal slur on their integrity or ability, or a claim being made against the firm which cannot be allowed to go unchallenged. Then flavour the whole thing with confusion about issues of negligence and what chance is there of approaching a complaint in a way the client will find acceptable.

Often it's not just confusing the issues of service and negligence, but rather approaching service complaints as if they were negligence claims.

A typical example of the sort of mentality that is all too pervasive occurred with the firm handling a divorce case on behalf of the respondent wife. She complained the firm had held onto her Petition for four months. What was the firm's reaction? They triumphantly pounced on the client's error to point out that she was the Respondent so they couldn't have held onto her petition. Did that solve the problem? Of course not. The fact was that the solicitors *had* held onto her Acknowledgement of Service for four months. It begs the question as to why the firm felt it necessary to be so pedantic when they must have known what the problem really was. They got their just desserts when the matter reached the OSS.

## WHAT DOES ALL THIS MEAN?

It means that when you come to deal with a complaint, you must:

- avoid reacting to it like a solicitor;
- reverse your normal thought processes and stop doing what comes naturally.

It actually takes a conscious effort to do it. You *must* be aware that you are doing.

If you are not, you won't be doing it.

# CHAPTER EIGHT
# HOW SHOULD CLIENTS BE ASKED TO COMPLAIN?

The answer is – in any way that the client wants to do it. One thing to be avoided is to require the client to put his complaints in writing as a pre-condition of having them addressed. The reason given for this by those who do so is invariably "it's the only way I can be sure I know what I have to deal with." Well, the truth of the matter is the direct opposite. In fact, very often, it is the only way you will *never* know what you are dealing with.

## WHY?

1.  Very often clients will put their complaints incorrectly. This is because the client will put his complaint as he perceives it, and, because he is unfamiliar with legal processes and procedures, he will often perceive it incorrectly and will then express it incorrectly. This, in turn, encourages the solicitor to dismiss the complaint as being groundless. This does nothing to resolve the problem and, in fact, only tends to make it worse because, as well as having a complaint, the client now feels he has been fobbed of into the bargain, which, in a sense, he has. This only makes him angrier and more deter-mined to do something about it, so he persists with his complaint, often insisting it has not been dealt with. The solicitor then perceives him as being a troublemaker, and so the whole thing spirals downwards.

2.  Not only are many people averse to having to do this, but it can be perceived as a barrier because the client is, in effect, being forced to have his complaint dealt with on the solicitor's terms, instead of on his own and, as a result, the client is going to resent it. That is when words like "arrogant" and "unapproachable" begin to be used. The client can all too easily form the view that the solicitor only wants things put in writing because he is better at it than the client is and advantage is being taken of his inferiority. Furthermore, clients can get so angry about this that by the time the complaint lands on your desk, it has grown out of all proportion, with the client throwing everything into his complaint that he can think of.

3.    It is, however, essential that the solicitor must agree with the client exactly what his complaints are or amount to. The complaint handler MUST find out what the complaint is all about. The last thing he wants to do is to spend time dealing with what he thinks are the complaints, only to find out after hours of patient work that he has been dealing with only half the complaints or even the wrong complaint entirely.

It is far easier done if the client is seen. Then the complaint handler can talk to the client who can be asked about the problem. If you are puzzled about the nature of the complaint or even if you do not understand it, there is a far better chance of your being able to work out what this is all about by talking to the client. You can then agree it with the client. The solicitor should then reduce it to writing and get the client to agree it and then everyone knows what is being dealt with. At the same time the client can be assured that you want to make sure that you are dealing with ALL his concerns and that you have correctly identified them. This will then stop the client coming back at a later date trying to add complaints or moving the goalposts and will enable you to politely decline to deal with the altered or additional complaints if he tries to do so.

Even if a client writes in with a complaint and says he is happy for it to be dealt with in writing, invite him into the office. This has several benefits. It enables the solicitor to more easily find out what is the real problem. It is the quickest way of dealing with an unhappy client – and the sooner the problem is addressed, the better the chance of resolving the matter. The client feels that the solicitor is concerned and is taking him seriously, and it is far more difficult for the client to be belligerent, than if it is all done on paper.

An example where the solicitors not only took the complaint at face value, but then, because the majority of what the client was complaining about seemed groundless, were dismissive about all the complaints occurred in a matter where the client complained she had never received a Client Care letter. This was also a case in which, had the complaint been spotted immediately, it could have been resolved very easily. Because it was not, by the time it reached the solicitors it had assumed frightening proportions.

The solicitor's response to the complaint was to produce a copy of the Client Care letter they had sent. It dealt with costs information, the identity and status of the fee-earner and the name of the partner to whom complaint could be made. The firm itself had dismissed the complaint, and the CCS caseworker was intrigued why the client still persisted with the complaint in the face of the evidence and decided to make further enquiry – something that the firm should have done themselves.

It transpired that what the client was really saying was that she had never received advice about the choices of action available to her and the file bore this out. There was no evidence that she had received any ongoing information at all; the issues had never been confirmed, nor how it was proposed to deal with them, nor was there any costs risk/benefit analysis.

Had the solicitors, faced with a client who persisted in her complaint in face of the apparently conclusive evidence to the contrary, taken the trouble to pursue further enquiries, preferably on a face-to-face basis, they could have found that out for themselves. Also, had the Rule 15 partner looked at the file with one eye on what *was not* there, rather than what *was* there, he could also have avoided the waste of time having to deal with the OSS, which then found against the firm into the bargain!

Incidentally, the reason the client described her complaint wrongly turned out to be that she had read a newspaper article saying solicitor had to give clients Client Care letters, but not explaining what they were. The client thought that must be what she had not had and complained accordingly. A stark example of just how easy it is for clients to get it wrong.

4. The fourth reason is that you must ensure that, whatever the outcome, the complaint is dealt with quickly. The quicker complaints are addressed, the easier they are to resolve. Do not, on any account, allow complaints to fester. If you do, they will just become all the harder, if not impossible, to resolve.

If you allow yourself to put off dealing with it, you are half way to ignoring it and more then half way to failing to resolve it.

Look at it from the client's viewpoint. He has a complaint and he is being ignored. What would your reaction be in similar circumstances? And it is even worse if one of the complaints is a failure to respond to letters and telephone calls!

A face-to-face meeting is best. If that is not practical or possible, use the telephone. Doing it all in writing is very much the last resort. It is the least accurate way, the slowest way and the most impersonal and affords the least chances of success.

5. Lastly, skilled though you may be at dealing with legal matters in writing, it is highly unlikely that skill will extend to dealing with complaints. It is virtually impossible for someone to write a letter to a complainant that he will find acceptable, particularly if the solicitor is disagreeing with him. When you are talking to someone you use body language and put stresses and accentuation on certain words to give them emphasis so they will know what you mean. You cannot do that in writing. The reader chooses the words that he wants to emphasise – and they may well not be the words that the author intended him to emphasise. Consequently the meaning can become blurred or ambiguous. What was intended as a nice, friendly letter can so easily come across as being argumentative or even patronising or condescending. Add to that the fact that the letter is being read by someone who is, in all probability, actually looking for double meanings or adverse inferences and the like, and what chance is there of writing something that cannot be misunderstood?

# CHAPTER NINE
# DEALING WITH THE COMPLAINT

## THE VITAL FIRST STEPS

There are certain essential steps that **must** be taken whenever a complaint is referred to the firm. The last thing that anyone can afford at this stage is to let the complaining client think that the firm is not interested in him or his complaint. Should he get that impression he will be lost totally and the firm is going to experience a long and traumatic time ahead.

It is essential also that the client does not perceive that there are barriers to his making a complaint and that any complaint is dealt with quickly. Look at it from the client's point of view. He has a concern that he wants to be resolved and he is being ignored. If you were the client what would your reaction be? It is also essential that the client feels he is being taken seriously. The complaint handler should also follow the following steps:

### No preconditions

Avoid imposing preconditions to the client making a complaint. The usual one is to require the complaint to be made in writing, as discussed in Chapter 8.

### Procedure on receipt

Therefore, it is imperative that, no matter what may be thought of the client or his complaint, the person to whom it is addressed absolutely **must, always**:

* Acknowledge receipt of the complaint by return of post

* Express concern that the client has found it necessary to complain

* Assure him that he will try to resolve his concerns, and, ideally,

* Invite the client to see him, if the complaint was made in writing.

If the complaint is absolutely clear, so that there is no possibility of error, and a personal meeting would be of no value, or is not practical, when the letter is sent, the client should be given a date by which the solicitor **knows**, beyond a shadow of doubt, that he can be in touch with the client again, adding three or four days for a safety margin. At this point, even if the client has not asked for it, it may be a good idea to give him a copy of the firm's Complaints Procedure, which should tell him **who** is going to do **what** and **when** it is going to do be done.

The next step is then to write to the client again *before the date which he had been given by which the next letter would be sent.*

### Agree the grounds of the complaint

No-one can start to deal with a complaint until they know for sure what it is all about.

As already indicated, don't dismiss the complaint *because* the client cannot explain it properly – that only aggravates the situation.

It is also essential to ensure that **all** the client's complaints are being dealt with simultaneously. The last thing anyone wants to do is to spend a lot of time on a complaint and to think it has been resolved, only for the client to say "That's all very well, but what about…?" It also avoids other complaints being added at a later date.

So, agree with the complainant the totality of the complaints and then confirm them in writing, but you, the solicitor, should do that! The client can then be asked to confirm your understanding. Agreement can be reached that what you have summarised represents *all* the complaints. If, then, at a later date, when the client does not like the conclusions reached and tries to move the goalposts by inventing further complaints, the solicitor would be justified in politely declining to deal with them, unless the new complaint reveals factors that the client could not possibly have known about earlier.

### Establish the redress sought

It is essential that it is known what the complainant wants to achieve by making the complaint. This gives a pointer as to the direction the matter will take and can save a lot of time. Remember, an apology costs nothing and can be given in an appropriate way even if the validity of the complaint is not accepted.

If a client has not indicated what he wants done to put matters right – ask him. If this is done, you may be surprised by some of the answers that you get. As already indicated it is entirely possible that it is not money. If it is not, then the complaint should be capable of a quick resolution. If it is, at least you know what you are up against.

Never forget that most complainants really want to have their concerns addressed in some meaningful way. They want to be taken seriously and to be treated sympathetically. Only when they do not get that kind of reaction do they start thinking in terms of compensation.

# THE PRACTICAL STEPS

1.  Invite the client into the office, if it is practical to do so and the client has not already been seen when he first indicated his complaint.
    This gives the client the impression he is being taken seriously and:

    - makes him more amenable
    - builds a personal rapport
    - enables you to get a better idea of the complaint
    - enables you to agree the issues involved, and
    - it is quicker than trying to do it all in writing.

    When seeing the client, go down to reception to meet him and escort him to where the meeting is to take place. Sit him down and make him comfortable. Offer him a cup of coffee. Ensure there are no artificial barriers between you. So do not have the client sitting opposite you on the other side of a desk. This immediately suggests a face-to-face confrontation. Ensure that your chair is not higher than the client's. Then, and most importantly, in the hearing and sight of the client, pick up the telephone and tell the telephonist that you are engaged in an important meeting and on no account are you to be disturbed. The fact that it isn't going to happen anyway is irrelevant – it is the impression which is being made on the client that is important. Finally, ensure that you have plenty of time.The whole effect will be ruined if you have to keep looking at your watch or if you have to terminate the meeting part way through because you have another client to see.

2.  Identify the Issues. This has already been partly covered **but** remember that clients can easily confuse issues because they know no different. Clients present complaints as they perceive them and are therefore prone to confuse, for example issues of delay with issues of failing to be kept informed, or issues of failing to follow instructions with failing to be kept informed.

3.  Examine the file. Complaints cannot be properly dealt with without doing so. When the file is examined, look out, not so much for what is

there, as for what is not there, but which should be. And remember, the client gets the benefit of the doubt.

If that is thought to be unfair, remember that it is the solicitor's job to record relevant matters, and also that the client will more likely than not, only have the one matter on, whilst the fee-earner will have a hundred or more. It is entirely possible, and indeed likely, that the fee-earner will say he has done something because that is what he usually does, whilst the client will have a better memory of what actually happened, or did not happen, in his particular case.

When examining the file, be objective and look, not only for evidence that relates directly to the complaint, but also for other possible explanations for what is bothering the client or things that should be recorded on the file, but are not.

Finally, of course, you should consult with the fee-earner, if only to get his observations on the conclusions that you reach from looking at the file.

4.    Then see the client again, prior to confirming to him, in writing, any conclusions which have been reached.

There can be two possible scenarios. Either:

- the complaint, or a part of it, is valid. If so, tell the client that in the letter inviting him to see you again. That will, at least, ensure that he comes in to the office in a proper frame of mind, or
- You disagree with the complaint. This is a more difficult situation to deal with. Do *not* tell the client, in the letter, of your conclusions. When he comes in, before he is told what conclusions have been reached, reiterate the complaints and then go through the evidence from the file, relating it to the complaints. When that has been done, ask the client whether **he** still thinks his complaints are valid. If he does, then go on to explain your own thinking and why you cannot agree with him.

Whatever the conclusions reached, confirm your own, with your reasoning and referring to the evidence where this can be done, **in writing**.

# THE GOLDEN RULES

## THE FIRST GOLDEN RULE: LISTEN

All of that has gone before about ascertaining what are the complaints and what the client is looking for in raising them with you involves the **first** golden rule, which is to **listen**, and this means "listen", not just "hear". Many are the complaints that have been made to the CCS that result from a solicitor not listening to his client in the first place. Do not repeat the fault when dealing with the resulting complaint.

There was a case that reached to OSS of an old lady whose husband had suddenly become violent towards her and who consulted her solicitors as a result. They did not listen to her, but heard what they wanted to hear and started off down the divorce route. The last thing the lady wanted was to get divorced, but, being elderly and not really understanding what was going on, (see Chapter Three, Part One) she signed the Petition.

Disaster was only averted when, after the matter had been set down, the husband went to consult solicitors of his own, who wrote asking if the long marriage could not be saved. At last the solicitors did something right and took instructions. The old lady was horrified to discover how close she had become to getting divorced. All she wanted was for something to be done to stop her husband from hitting her.

When first seeing the client who has a complaint, let him get it off his chest, particularly if he is angry. *Do not interrupt* – that will be interpreted by the client as your wanting to argue with him and this will only make him even angrier. Be assured that, eventually, the client will run out of steam, particularly if nothing more happens that has the result of winding him up, so that there is nothing to feed his spleen.

At the very least, interruptions will be interpreted as disinterest or failing to take the client and his complaint seriously. The sort of reaction it produces can be gauged by an extract from a letter received by the OSS from a complainant which read as follows:

> "I tried to explain this (to the solicitor) in our telephone conver-
> sation...and he refused to listen to me. He butted in to everything I
> was trying to say and wouldn't let me finish a sentence. He was
> clearly not listening to a single word."

All that is needed at this stage are signs that you are listening and taking in what is said. When you are talking to the client, or listening to him, take notes – just jot down headings – and let the client see that you are doing so. This shows that you are listening, are interested and helps you to identify the areas of complaint. The occasional nodding of the head or non-committal grunt at the appropriate stage will suffice.

Then, when the client has calmed down a little, seek to agree with him what his complaints are. This reassures the client that he is, at least, being taken seriously.

Remember, as was pointed out earlier, the client may not really know, in technical terms, what his complaints amount to and it is all too easy to take advantage of that and to dismiss the complaints as being groundless. However, that will not resolve the problem or make it go away. The client may just have a gut feeling that something is wrong, but cannot put his finger on the problem. If that is the case, then talk to him and get him to talk to you and try to draw him out. Eventually you will be able to identify his concerns.

Do not cross-examine the client. Again that will be taken as being confrontational. It is very easy to do, so care needs to be taken. For example, if you really want to question what the client has said, it is fatal to say something like "Are you sure that...?" Not unnaturally, the client interprets that as meaning "I don't think you can be right about that". In other words, you are doubting what he says and, depending on how his mood is, he may accuse you of calling him a liar! Now he is wound up again, and off he will go, subjecting you to another thirty minutes harangue.

It is far better to say something like "Can you tell me a bit more about....?" if necessary, specifying the exact area of concern.

## THE SECOND GOLDEN RULE: AVOID CONFRONTATION

The **second** of the golden rules, as may be anticipated, is **don't be confrontational** (or aggressive or defensive or even dismissive).

This, regrettably, is more difficult than one may suppose and is something that most solicitors clearly find difficult, and, in some cases, impossible. (That sentence itself is, in fact, confrontational – not in what is said, but in the way it is said – all will become clear later!)

The conceptual side of this has already been dealt with in Chapter 7, so let us have a look at the more practical side.

One response to a complaint made by a litigation lawyer was typical. Having said what the firm had done, he continued "...I would argue that..." Can there be any phrase more calculated to give the wrong message or more guaranteed to produce an argument where one is not wanted?

It is almost as if solicitors, even when they recognise that service has fallen short of acceptable standards, fight shy of admitting it, possibly because they think that any admission may, in some way, be to their prejudice in the future. This merely leaves the client with a sense of outrage and only strengthens their resolve to do something about it.

A typical example of this occurred in the case of a firm against whom a complaint had been made in a divorce matter. Here the firm committed those cardinal errors outlined above.

The client had consulted the solicitors when a divorce petition was issued against her. The solicitors advised her that her only bargaining tool with regard to financial matters was her ability to delay the grant of the Decree Absolute to her husband, who was keen to re-marry, and she accordingly instructed her solicitors to do whatever was necessary in order to best protect her interests. The solicitor had suggested that this could be done by making an application to the court and he was thereupon instructed to make the application.

Unfortunately, the solicitor completely forgot to do so and the husband obtained his Decree Absolute before the financial affairs were settled, and the husband was then able to drag matters out for another two years before the client lost patience and instructed another firm.

When the final Order had been made, the client complained that her original solicitors had failed to follow her instructions and, indeed, the advice that they themselves had given her. The Complaints Partner at the firm complained of, acknowledged the advice the firm had given, the instructions they had received and the firm's omission in complying with those instructions. He went on to acknowledge the stress and frustration caused to the client as a result, but then made the classic mistake of observing that, as it did not appear that the client had lost out financially, and may even have obtained a better Order than she would have done had the matter been promptly pursued to a conclusion, there was no reason for the firm to make any financial concession to her.

This was a classic example of a solicitor treating a service complaint as if it was a negligence claim and looking at the material loss to the client in order to determine the complaint's validity. This is all the more remarkable as the solicitor recognised the frustration and stress the inadequacy had caused the client, but then dismissed those factors as being irrelevant in determining the validity of the complaint when, in fact, they were the *only* determining factors.

Needless to say, the OSS took a different view and ordered the firm to pay their client compensation.

To resolve complaints successfully solicitors **must** stop doing what comes naturally. This means that when a complaint is received the solicitor has to make a conscious effort not to react as if this was another client who has come to see him with a problem on which he is seeking advice. Instead, that conscious effort needs directing towards appreciating that here is an unhappy client, finding out what it is that has created that unhappiness and taking any necessary remedial action. If, having considered the matter properly, it is considered that the client was mistaken, the solicitor should, by that stage, still know what caused the client's unhappiness and be able to patiently explain to the client why his perception is wrong. And do not forget, that often what is wrong is that the client is unhappy because it is his own expectations that have not been met and nothing was done at the outset to discover what those expectations were and correct any that were considered to be unreasonable – and that *is* the fault of the solicitor.

Also bear in mind that, often, senior partners do not always make the best complaint partners. Indeed, they may only have become senior partner because they **are** confrontational by nature.

Consider an extract from a letter one disgruntled complainant wrote to the senior partner of his solicitors' firm.

The background was that the client had had an assistant solicitor acting for him. He had a minor concern that he mentioned to the assistant who was in course of resolving the matter quite satisfactorily as far as the client was concerned when the senior partner, opening the post one morning, noticed a reference to it in a letter and insisted he take over.

One can guess what followed from this extract from a letter the client eventually wrote.

> "I would conclude by stating that your firm started out as our ally and, because of your attitude, has now become our enemy. A fine state of affairs and I hope you are pleased with yourself. Needless to say, your firm's name is mud in our household and we will have no hesitation in making this fact known to our wide circle of friends and business acquaintances."

I also include in this category the tendency to be dismissive, which, in itself, does nothing except aggravate the complainant.

The very worst thing that can occur is the abrupt dismissal.

Consider one solicitor's response to a complaint:

> "Having looked into this file, I can assure you that the fee-earner concerned followed normal procedures and could not be criticised for the legal steps that were taken on your behalf."

That was it!

Quite apart from the fact that the solicitor was making that all too common mistake and was treating this as a complaint about the standard of workmanship and not the standard of service, there was no mention of the specific items of concern that the client had raised and also completely ignored the rather inconvenient fact that it had taken the fee-earner just short of three years to complete a job that, in all conscience, should have taken no longer than nine months.

It is this type of reply that points up the problem, as has been already mentioned, of the confusion, even in the minds of solicitors, between issues of negligence and service.

Maybe, in this case, the solicitor did not know the difference, but the likelihood is that he was only looking at the complaint from the point of view of a potential negligence claim being made. From the words used, it is a reasonable conclusion to make that he had one eye on defending such a claim.

Being non-confrontational is more difficult than one may think. It is perfectly possible for anyone to dictate a letter that they *think* sounds conciliatory and neutral in tone, but which *reads* totally differently to the person receiving it. Let's be frank – it is far from easy to write letters, particularly those that disagree with the complainant, that are going to be regarded by the recipient as being acceptable. Such letters need to be carefully thought out. Every line and word needs to be carefully considered, the constant criterion being "is there a better way to say this?"

Firstly, ensure that the client is not put off reading the letter, so set it out with short paragraphs, with a space between each. This makes it much easier to read and is far less intimidating than looking at two closely typed pages. Everyone must know, from personal experience, how daunting that can be.

Then, pay attention to the length of the sentences you are using. This may not seem important, but it is, because their length creates an impression in the reader's mind.

If sentences are too long, there is a tendency for the message that it is sought to express to become obscured. Everyone knows how difficult and frustrating it is to try to understand the provisions of some statutes that ramble on for nine or ten lines with scarcely a verb to be seen. If a complainant receives a letter like that, his reaction is going to be that you are trying to hide something and are trying to baffle him with science.

On the other hand, letters that contain sentences that are too short and staccato come over as being aggressive and distinctly unfriendly – which should be just what you are trying to avoid.

Next, pay attention to the actual words that are being used. Generally speaking, if a response to a complaint is being dictated and it is suddenly realised that the words or phrases that are being used slip off the tongue all too easily, then beware. This is because they are words and phrases that you habitually use in dealing with your daily work and because you are not *really* thinking about what you are saying. The almost inevitable consequence is that what you are saying will not be put in a way that is acceptable to the complainant. What is more, there is a distinct danger that what is dictated will be ungrammatical, so that, even if what is said would have been otherwise acceptable, it is rendered unacceptable – a mistake which is only magnified when the letter is signed off without even being read!

Ensure plain English is used. As mentioned in Part One, avoid big words e.g. "axiomatic" or "peripatetic", or legal phraseology e.g. "hereinbefore referred to".

Even when every word used has been carefully considered, it is still necessary to go back again over the completed letter and reconsider what has been said, asking oneself whether there is any way that what has been said can be misconstrued, not just in what has been said, but in its tone. It is not a bad idea to ask one of the non-lawyers in the office (not your own secretary who can be too close to the complaint) to read the letter and ask them to tell you what their reaction would be if they received that letter in response to a complaint. What you are looking for is not criticism of the content, but how the letter comes across.

Be wary of those who will say it is good just because you are a partner and that is what they think you want to hear. Assure them it is not and that you really want to know how it reads.

When you are happy that you have got it right, put the letter in your desk drawer, lock it and leave it there until the next day. Then get it out and read it again. You may be amazed at the perception you will then have of what you wrote the day before, and I would guess that there will be several changes you will make to the phraseology, even if you don't scrap the whole thing and start all over again!

Sadly, even when all this has been done, it is a fact that you still will not please everyone all the time. One of the problems is that a word can be dictated using a particular inflection in the voice, but letters do not reproduce inflections and, consequently, the recipient of the letter may put an interpretation on it that was not intended.

Always remember that responding to complaints in an appropriate way is an art-form in itself and something that does not come naturally to most people, let alone lawyers whose lifetime has been spent dealing with issues in a way that is very far removed from that necessary to resolve dissatisfaction.

Of one thing you can be sure – if the complaint "escapes" and gets to the stage where the client is becoming intractable, if it is possible to interpret a word in two different ways, it will be interpreted in the way that was not intended. Even the most innocuous phrase will be subject to scrutiny by a suspicious mind that is looking for hidden meanings and if it's possible to be misinterpreted, then it will be.

That is one of the main reasons why it is better to try to resolve complaints on a face-to-face basis, rather than just attempt to do it in writing.

One of the main things to remember in order to avoid being confrontational is to **avoid adverbs like the plague** or phrases that amount to adverbs. Remember, earlier it was indicated that a particular sentence was confrontational? What was said was that being non-confrontational was "clearly something that most solicitors find difficult." The reference was to the use of the word "clearly".

It must be constantly borne in mind that adverbs are perceived, particularly by someone who is lodging a complaint, as being confrontational. They are potentially lethal to successful complaints handling

There is a great temptation to use them, particularly for emphasis, but the temptation *must* be resisted. It can be almost guaranteed that anyone, dictating a letter that disagrees with a complaint will, at some stage or other find themselves automatically using an adverb. Be on the look-out for it and dismiss the idea immediately.

"Clearly" or "obviously", or phrases having the same meaning, are the favourites. Say something like "clearly it is the case that..." or "It is clear that..." and the almost predictable and inevitable reaction will be "well it might be clear to you, mate, but it isn't clear to me, and, if it's clear to you, why didn't you explain it to me properly in the first place?"

Another word that is even worse and which can almost be guaranteed to provoke fury and allegations that the solicitor is being patronising is "frankly". And, in terms of successful complaints handling, being patronising is even worse than being confrontational or defensive.

The second type of expression that has to be avoided at all costs is those clever little put-down phrases that those in the law tend to love. "With respect..." because even the dumbest client knows that you mean exactly the opposite. And "I hear what you say..." but I haven't the slightest intention of taking any notice of you!

Everyone who deals with complaints, at whatever level, must be constantly alert to guard against using such words, because, believe me, you *will* catch yourself using them! If only that one lesson is remembered, a big step towards successfully resolving complaints will have been made.

Apart from not being confrontational, what are the other golden rules for successful complaints handling?

## THE THIRD GOLDEN RULE: DON'T BLAME THE CLIENT

This is all too easy to do, particularly in divorce cases where the client can easily be perceived as having their views coloured and distorted by his or her personal problems and by thinking that the complaint merely reflects the client's own troubled personal life.

It is also easy to do when the client has totally unreasonable expectations. When these complaints are analysed they demonstrate the gulf that exists in the understanding by the client on the one hand and the solicitor on the other, of such basic issues as what was going to be achieved and by when. Solicitors often fail to appreciate their client's perspective on these issues and the client, in turn, fails to understand what is going on.

The result is that the solicitor *thinks* the client knows what is going on. The client raises no query or objection at the time and the solicitor then fails to recognise as legitimate any complaints expressed at a later date.

Blaming the client is also the almost automatic reaction to complaints that arise when the solicitor has made a mistake in accounting to the client and overpays them, and then, sometime later has to write asking the client to repay the money overpaid. I have known some spectacular instances, the worst being an overpayment of some £9,000 that went unnoticed for thirteen months! The common reaction is to say that the client didn't check the Completion Statement etc. This completely ignores the fact that it is the solicitor's job to get the Statement right (that is part of what he is being paid for) and it is not the client's job to check the solicitor has done his properly.

Remember, you, the solicitor, are the expert and the client is relying on you. Basically, if the client gets something wrong, it could well be because you, the solicitor, have not explained it properly.

Putting the blame back on the client is easily done, and can be done quite unwittingly. By way of illustration, consider this quotation from the draft of a seminar prepared by a professional Course presenter. Remember, this man was supposed to be an expert who was giving this as his model example of how a solicitor should respond to a complaint.

What the draft said was "Having looked into the matter, I can see that you could easily have been confused by the steps that were taken..."

Do you see what those words are doing? In effect, the client is being blamed for being confused. In other words, it is telling the client he is incapable of understanding! It doesn't matter if he is – you can't tell that to the client. And, anyway it is no excuse. You should have realised the client was "thick" and ensured that he understood your explanation.

Any complaining client, reading that would be quite likely, and understandably, to hit the proverbial roof.

What the letter should have said would have been something like "I now appreciate that matters could, and should, have been explained to you more clearly and I apologise for the fact that they were not."

## THE FOURTH GOLDEN RULE: KEEP AN OPEN MIND

This, again, unfortunately, is something which is easy to say but difficult to put in practice and with which many solicitors seem to find difficulty, probably because it is interpreted as only meaning that one should admit fault if it exists. That certainly is part of it, but it goes much farther than that. In fact, the word "fault" is too strong, but if you know something could have been done better, don't be shy of saying so – it could be all the client wants to hear.

Keeping an open mind really involves, not merely being willing to admit fault if it exists, but going further and being ready to look behind how the complaint is actually presented to see if there are wider implications which may not have been apparent to the complainant and therefore not mentioned by him, but, nevertheless, were probably the underlying factor which induced the complaint which was made.

As mentioned earlier, many clients either cannot properly express their complaints, or, pick the wrong issue to complain about.

Reference has already been made to the fact that complaints of delay often turn out to be complaints of failing to keep the client informed. That is to say, for example, knowing that nothing would happen for some time, the solicitor fails to tell the client, or, when, unexpectedly, nothing has happened for some time, he fails to tell the client why. Either way the client perceives the issue as one of delay simply because if he is not told that there is a reason for nothing happening, he assumes, reasonably enough, that the matter has been overlooked, and that is what he complains about.

Similar considerations apply to complaints that a solicitor has failed to follow instructions when the fact of the matter is that the solicitor had very good reasons for not doing as he was asked but has omitted to tell the client those reasons.

In either case, if the Rule 15 Partner adopts the narrow approach and looks at the complaint literally as expressed by the client, he will conclude there was no delay for which the firm could be blamed, or that there were perfectly good reasons why particular instructions were not followed, and he then dismisses the complaint. The result of both of these scenarios is that the client still remains dissatisfied and takes the matter further. The solicitor is then surprised when the client goes to the CCS to whom he expresses righteous indignation at the slur on the good name of his firm.

He will, predictably, be even more surprised and indignant when a finding of inadequacy of service is made against his firm because they failed to tell the client of the reasons for the several periods of weeks and months when nothing happened, or why the solicitor did something different to what the client wanted, and there was no explanation from the firm.

This could easily have been avoided if the Rule 15 Partner had adopted a more open- minded approach and taken a broader view, and, realised that, while the client was unhappy, he may not have properly understood the true reasons for that unhappiness. Had the Rule 15 partner kept an open mind, he would have perceived that the real cause of complaint was not, in fact, delay, but the fact that the client was kept in the dark about why nothing had happened for some time without him being warned or told why. He would have realised that the complaint was really that the client was not kept informed, and *that*, as a ground for complaint, *was* justified and he should have done something to resolve it.

These types of complaint are prime examples of the difficulties that can arise when a solicitor takes the complaint too literally and adopts a narrow view. There are many other examples and anyone handling complaints should be on the look-out for them.

As mentioned briefly earlier, it involves adopting an approach which enables you to recognise the existence of an inadequacy of service where no actual complaint has been made about it, but which may be the underlying cause of the complaint which has been made.

A typical example of this kind of thing arrived at the OSS in March 2000. The letter is reproduced below. Read it and before going further, decide for yourself what it was that was *really* troubling the client and what the complaints actually amounted to.

"In April 1997 I had a car accident. I have had no less than 4 different names to contact in those 'nearly' three years. Now I have a Mr Smith. I was last talking to him after a silence of 4+ months & numerous messages left on his voice-mail for an update. He was to contact me on 28 Feb, but nothing. I am concerned about the results of my MRI scan which proved to be more serious than I had been led to believe by two private doctors. The last I heard was that the other solicitors were getting my medical history sent to them in May 1999. Now nothing again. I am constantly chasing."

What do you make of that?

This was the solicitor's response.

> "We appreciate your frustration that your case has been allocated to four different fee-earners since we were first instructed. This was necessary as the previous handlers dealing with your claim are no longer with us.
>
> In relation to the number of messages left on Mr Smith's voice-mail, he does not recall receiving a number of messages, but, if this is the case he apologises for failing to return the calls.
>
> In your conversation with Mr Smith on 17 February, he confirms that he arranged to call you the following day but failed to do so as he had not noted his file to telephone you. Please accept his sincere apologies.
>
> We note your comments with regard to your recent MRI scan. We confirm we have received a copy of the other party's medical expert's report and enclose a copy of the same for your perusal and comment.
>
> As you are aware, liability in this matter is firmly in dispute on the grounds…(at this point the letter went on to set out the two different versions of the accident)…There were no independent witnesses and we feel that…it is likely a Judge would believe the other side's case to be stronger and award judgment in their favour.
>
> In the light of the above we do not feel there are reasonable prospects in making recovery of your losses. We are under a duty to your Legal Expense Insurers to ensure that you have reasonable prospects of recovery and we would not be fulfilling our duty either to yourself or your insurer if we allowed the claim to continue… ."

The solicitors were then surprised at the client's reaction, which was to accuse them of trying to fob her off and just get rid of her and that they had not even begun to address her concerns.

The change of fee-earner and the failure to return her calls were the obvious complaints, but they were the immediate cause for the complaint being raised and were the tip of the iceberg. What the complainant was really concerned about was the delay and the lack of information she had been getting, and, of course, the solicitor's letter did nothing to address those issues. Anyone looking at the complainant's letter with an open mind should have picked up what the probable real causes of the complaints were, looked at the file with them in mind and then addressed them in their response to the client.

What made matters worse in this case was, of course, the unwelcome news that the solicitors were only now imparting to the complainant, with only a month of the limitation period to run. Even then, their letter failed to mention the limitation implications. Is it any wonder that, far from resolving the complainant's concerns, the letter only served to inflame the whole issue – a perfect example of how not to do it!

It is entirely possible that, before you can start to deal with a complaint, you may have to seek further, more specific, information from the client. This happens particularly when complaints are expressed in general terms. In such cases, you will have to gently explain to the client that you cannot really deal with concerns which are only expressed in general terms, such as a failure to keep him informed about progress in his case. Explain to him that you need to know what it is that he says has happened and about which he should have been told, that he was not.

It may be that he says that he was never told anything (and in some cases that is found to be true!), in which case, he can be nothing but general in the expression of his concerns. However, usually it is some specific event or two about which the complainant thinks he ought to have been told, but was not.

Likewise, a suggestion that the client's instructions were not followed is not precise enough. To deal with such a complaint, it is necessary to know what instructions the client says he gave, that were then ignored.

Sometimes, when solicitors deny the validity of a complaint, it is not that they are devious or dishonest. It is that they just cannot bring themselves to admit that there is even the faintest of possibilities that they, or their partners or employees, are less than perfect.

Do ensure that you do not adopt the automatic denial syndrome. Do not, under any circumstances, start off with the reaction "This complaint cannot be right. Harry would never have forgotten to do that." If you do, you are more than half way towards failing to resolve the complaint before you ever start. Before you have made any kind of investigation, you are already convinced that the complaint is spurious. It is entirely possible that, in this instance, Harry did forget it! How many times have you maintained you have done something because you are in the habit of doing it that way, only to find out later that you didn't put the key back in its box, after all?

# CHAPTER TEN
# PRACTICAL EXAMPLES: HOW NOT TO DO IT

It may now be the appropriate time to look at one or two practical examples of how **not** to handle complaints in order to illustrate the kinds of thing that should be avoided.

## Case one

The background to the first was a complaint by a beneficiary who was unhappy about some aspect of the interest that had been earned on estate assets and had written to the solicitor with her query.

In these examples, only the names have been changed to protect the guilty, but the wording, in each example, is accurately quoted.

---

**A.N. TAGONISTIC**

Solicitor
Confrontation House
Stroppy Square
Grumpstown

Dear Mrs Whingebucket

*Re Estate of A Deadman decd*

We would be obliged if you would inform this office of what you are not aware of in relation to the deposit interest. We wrote to each and every beneficiary last year and we enclose copy letter herewith. We also advised you as to what the sum was and this has been credited to the Estate. These matters are placed in the Estate accounts and we are at a loss to ascertain just exactly what it is that you are not made aware.

We would be obliged if you would telephone this office to communicate with us what the information is you require. It may be also courtesy to this office to advise us on what it is you say you perhaps have and that there is an absence of the information you require.

May we respectfully remind you that every beneficiary apart from yourself seems to accept the situation, quite happy with how we have conducted matters. I cannot understand what your problem is and therefore cannot assist unless you advise of such.

Yours sincerely

---

One can see here the undisguised irritation of the solicitor in having to deal with this query, which, at that time was not a complaint, but which was soon to become one!

The better response would surely have been something on the following lines.

> "I have your letter with regard to deposit interest earned on the assets of the above estate while the monies have been held by this office, but I regret to say that I do not fully understand the query you are raising.
>
> I had hoped that my letter of..............., which I sent to each beneficiary, would have explained the calculations and I am not sure whether it is the method of calculation which is causing you the problem or some other consideration.
>
> Perhaps the quickest way in which the problem can be resolved would be for you to come and see me and perhaps you may like to telephone my secretary to arrange an appointment when it would be convenient for you call at the office for that purpose. If a personal visit is impractical, please telephone and I will try to deal with your concerns in that way, although I would prefer to see you in person if that is possible.
>
> I look forward to hearing from you."

## Case two

The background to the next complaint was that it arose in respect of a failure by the solicitor to account for deposit interest earned. Again, the solicitor's annoyance is all too clear.

The details of the complaint are irrelevant, save to say that the complainant had a genuine query.

However, she was one of those people who was particular and who wanted to know everything and this had apparently irritated the solicitor, so that his own responses got more and more brusque and, consequently, the client's requests became more and more insistent.

The complainant brought the matter to the OSS and, as it did not appear that she had formally raised his complaint with the solicitor under Rule 15 a telephone call was made to the complaints partner who gave an assurance that if details of the complaint were sent to him, he would deal with it and sort it out.

Knowing that the OSS knew about the matter and that it would become fully involved if the matter was not resolved, the solicitor's response was unbelievable.

---

I M Clueless & Co                                           29 October 1998
Solicitors

Dear Mrs..........................

I have your letter of ...................... which does not surprise me, in view of your rudeness throughout this entire transaction, you having made frequent, rude and insulting telephone calls to my office.

I look forward to documentary evidence in support of your claim for £240 extra interest for the non-return of a cheque, which is not, in any event, admitted.

You will indeed be paid whatever is due to you under the Deposit Interest Rules at the end of October.

As to the rest of your allegations, I repeat that you were so rude throughout this entire transaction that you may recall being invited to take your account elsewhere on at least one occasion, but you chose not to do that.

That was, of course, deliberate, because you always intended to make this claim from the beginning, and the claim is, of course, to that extent bogus.

Your allegations of professional misconduct are not accepted, but I am not surprised to receive them, in view of your behaviour throughout, which was appallingly rude.

Yours sincerely

---

Significantly, the solicitor's letter was written on 29 October. Note the third paragraph!

The complainant then, not having received anything further from the solicitor by 14 November, wrote to the OSS again, now complaining of the solicitor's "brash attitude" and saying "I do not understand their attitude to me, as you said in your letter to me that they would resolve the problem, not make it worse. Why are they doing this?"

A question one may well ask, particularly as the solicitor had now aggravated the problem by utterly failing to keep their promise to account to the client. Suffice it to say that the subsequent letter from the OSS to the solicitor was couched in suitably forthright terms.

## Case three

The next one is more subtle. It is not phrased so blatantly inappropriately as the others. The writer was at least making an effort, but, looking at it as a whole, one can appreciate, perhaps, just how difficult it is to get it right.

The background is that the client had complained that the solicitors, who, he said, had missed heads of claim out of his compensation claim, had also failed to respond to queries raised on his behalf by his Insurance Brokers and had then delayed in accounting to him, causing him extra expense because he had to extend his Bank overdraft to meet the shortfall.

---

*Ivor Problem*
Solicitor
Mindblock House

Dear Mr Smith

We cannot and do not accept what you say Mr Brown of X & Co has informed you. All communications both verbal and written were answered.

You say the cost of delay of receiving your cheque was £667.67. You further say that the documentation supplied shows this. However, we regret to advise that we cannot see how you have arrived at this and should be grateful if you could please kindly elucidate if you wish us to consider this point further.

In respect of the bill supplied by your brokers, we consider this as something that has been simply fabricated to inflate the amount of your compensation claim against us.

You have not produced any evidence that you are liable to pay this account.

We liaised with you on a regular basis and you were well aware that we were waiting a cheque from the third party. When this was received, we forwarded it to you without waiting for it to clear. There can be no allegation that we delayed payment to you. The delay was outside our control. All we could do was chase continually and which we did.

You indicate we agreed to pay the time spent with your broker... please refer back to our letter... when we indicated we would 'consider' the items mentioned... Given that...only...£205.80 of your settlement monies related to out-of-pocket expenses... we would have expected that money used for day to day expenses (would) have been diverted to pay for your accident expenses... leaving you short to pay your normal expenses. We are wondering how the bank charges accrued as they do not seem to be directly attributable to any delays... in receiving your settlement monies....

We are not prepared to consider any... amount unless we receive advices suggesting as to reconsider."

---

The wording is accurately quoted. Bad English does not help. What kind of impression does that letter make on you?

In this case the writer thought he had got it right and that the message in his letter was perfectly reasonable. But what did the client make of it?

His response read "Their letter (has) left me very stunned...an apology would have been nice, but to be talked down to is unacceptable."

## Case four

And, now, a very good example of how difficult it is to rid oneself of ingrained habits and to introduce totally the wrong atmosphere into the relationship with the client. Be honest – how many letters have you written which are couched in similar terms?

The background is that the solicitors had sent a settlement cheque to the client. He considered it was for the wrong amount and tried, unsuccessfully, to speak to the solicitors about it. He then spoke to the third party insurers who had issued the cheque. They advised him to return it to his solicitors. He did so, and, having heard nothing more for some weeks, wrote to the solicitors enquiring why. Their reply was:

---

**I.M. STROPPY**
*Solicitor*

Dear Mr Client

I thank you for your letter of 10 October last, the contents of which I note.

In my letter to you of 23 September I indicated that I could not have traced having received back from you our client account cheque representing your settlement monies.

Might this be because you sent it to Mr Bloggs at Commercial Union following your telephone conversation with him when he suggested you return the cheque.

I would be grateful if you could please kindly let me know to whom you did in fact return the cheque....

---

Again, the phraseology is quoted accurately, and, of course, does nothing to assist. However, is it not possible to detect the undertones of aggravation and the development of what is shortly destined to become a full-blown confrontation? Even the word "kindly" takes on sarcastic undertones, when, almost certainly, it was not intended that way and serves to illustrate the point about words slipping off the tongue all too easily, simply because the writer was not really thinking about what he was saying.

Would it not have been possible to write something on the lines of:

"I regret that I cannot trace having received your letter in which you say you enclosed the cheque. Is it possible to check that the letter was correctly addressed to us? If you could also let us know the time, date and place of posting we will make enquiries of the postal authorities as we are concerned what may have become of it. In the meantime, we will stop payment of the cheque and issue you with a replacement."

And I haven't even commented on the propriety, or otherwise, of paying a cheque made payable to the client into the firm's Client Account!

## Case five

Then, consider this example.

This letter was not written in response to a complaint. It was written during the normal course of the progress of a claim when the third party insurers queried some aspects of the claim being made.

Whilst the letter has been edited, the salient parts have been left in. What impression does it make upon you, the reader? Even more to the point, what impression would it make upon you if you received such a letter as a client?

> "The Third Party Insurers are not prepared to make any offers in respect of the outstanding heads of claim...I have been involved in lengthy correspondence (with them)...The outstanding matters include a Physiotherapist's invoice for a report . Kindly advise why you incurred this additional expense. Clearly (it) does not relate to costs incurred for treatment.
>
> Your claim includes a claim for lost earnings. You have provided a manuscript hand-written note...Clearly we will need better documentation in support. Please provide wage slips for 13 weeks prior to the accident.
>
> With regard to the Storage Account, an Engineer's inspection was arranged on 4 September at your (home). There is no reference to any Storage Account and ...the vehicle has clearly been stored at your premises...We advised that you obtain a pro-forma invoice from White's. You subsequently obtained a report from Black's dated 7 December....The report refers to a Storage Account accruing at Green's, but no confirmation of this from Green's is attached.
>
> We will need clarification as to why you accrued a Storage Charge from 7 December to 29 January. Clearly you have disregarded the advice offered in the engineer's report, which confirms your vehicle to be a write-off and that "the vehicle is moved from their premises as soon as possible to minimise any further charges being entailed." Please also advise why a Storage Account was accrued in any event given that when our instructed engineer inspected your vehicle it was stored at your premises.
>
> Please advise why the suggestions raised in our letter of 15 October were disregarded and why you obtained a further report from Black's. Furthermore, why was the vehicle stored at Green's?
>
> We await hearing from you."

Now, it would be correct to say that all the points that the solicitor was making were valid and required explanation, but the letter is written in a totally inappropriate, but, regrettably, all too familiar, way.

Bear in mind this is a solicitor writing to his own client, whose cause he is supposed to be supporting. However, instead of writing the letter in a way that seeks to find out why the client has apparently done things that, at first sight, seem inexplicable and to explain to him why it is necessary to have proper documentary support for claims that are made, the letter is written as though the solicitors are acting for the party against whom the claim is being made.

If that is the way that this solicitor writes to his client, one can be forgiven for wondering what on earth the letters are like that he writes in response to a complaint.

The whole tone of the letter is that the solicitor wants to argue with the client. Four times the word "clearly" is used, when it should not appear even once! In fact that letter is a very good example of the reason why the use of such adverbs, as indicated above, should be avoided at all costs. They, more than any other factor, set the whole tone for the letter.

One can fairly safely conclude, as was the case, that a complaint followed very soon after the despatch of the letter in question!

## Case six

The next example is a perfect illustration of not just how one can go "over the top" in reacting to what was not even a letter of complaint, but also in utterly failing to appreciate the client's concerns – typical of the response of someone under pressure.

The client was involved in a sale and purchase in which it was taking an age to get contracts exchanged – so long that her sellers had threatened to pull out and put their property back on the market. The fault did not lie with the solicitors, but with her buyer's surveyors who were taking an unconscionable length of time to produce their survey report, and she knew that.

The crux came when the day the fee-earner dealing with her transactions went on holiday – the very day that the survey finally came through and her buyer was ready to proceed. She heard nothing for a week, which bothered her because she thought that although the fee-earner was away, the urgency was known and surely someone will pick it up and do something. After a week's silence she telephoned the firm and spoke to someone who was, shall we say, less than helpful, so she wrote a letter to the firm. Still a further week went by with nothing happening, so she wrote the following letter addressed to the senior partner.

"Further to my letter of 17 August, I would like to inform you that I am becoming frustrated with the service that I am receiving from you.

The matter of the lease of my property has now been going on for four months and is looking likely to result in the loss of my purchase of....

I am aware that the majority of the delay is due to the surveyors, but I am most frustrated that no response has been given to their letter of 7 August, and, when I telephoned, your stand-in, while you were on holiday, informed me you do not know how to go about this matter. This left me very frustrated and upset.

Please could you give this matter your utmost priority as I want to speed up this process as quickly as possible."

Now, that is not a letter of complaint. It is someone writing expressing justified concern that nothing is happening, worried about losing her purchase and asking for someone to do something. However, it prompted this response from the senior partner.

"Thank you for your letter of 24 August. I have to say that I am very disappointed in your attitude and I would respectfully remind you that Miss X has been on her annual holiday over the last two weeks, as you are well aware.

I understand your frustration and concern at possibly losing your purchase. I am satisfied from looking at the file that Miss X has dealt with the matter entirely properly throughout and I do not believe that either she or this firm deserves criticism such as that contained in your last letter.

I believe in this case that your criticism is quite unwarranted and unless it is withdrawn I propose that we would both be better served if you were to transfer your instructions to another firm.

Such a course of action would not necessarily speed things up as they too may have staff who take a holiday, Nevertheless, unless you withdraw the criticism contained in your last letter, I will be instructing Miss X to prepare an account for work done to date and you will be invited to settle this account and take your files to a new solicitor.

P.S. This letter is being dictated and typed at 10.30pm as I and several other members of staff are working late to do what we can to cover for staff holidays."

Well, what a public relations disaster that is!

Firstly, there was no criticism, certainly not of Miss X, so it could hardly be withdrawn. Then he says he understands the client's frustration and concern and then goes on to demonstrate that he has not the slightest understanding of it at all. The sarcasm, particularly in the postscript, is unwarranted and completely unacceptable. If he has a problem covering for staff on holiday, that is his problem – it is not the client's.

## Case seven

However, bad though that may be it really pales into insignificance with the last example, which surely must rank as the worst response to a complaint ever made. It defies belief that any solicitor could respond to a complaint in such a way – even if he did believe it to be totally unjustified.

The background was that the client had lived with his partner for many years. They had had a child, but had had their differences and separated. There many aspects to be resolved, but the client's most immediate concern was that his ex-partner had stopped him seeing his son, so he had made an application for a contact order. It was taking an age to get a court hearing date. The problem lay, not with the solicitors, but with the welfare services who were taking far too long to prepare their Report. However, the solicitors had not told the client that. Looking at things from his point of view, he was paying the solicitors to get the matter into court so, if it was taking too long, it was their responsibility.

He decided to send in to the firm a Complaint Resolution Form, which he had obtained. This gives space for the complaint, which in his case was relatively simple – this is taking too long – and at the bottom there are two boxes and the client is asked to tick the appropriate box. One says 'I am happy for you to deal with my complaint in writing' and the alternative is 'I would prefer you to arrange a meeting to discuss my complaint.' The relevance of that will soon become clear.

The solicitors actual letter in reply was one line long:

> "Dear Mr Smith, We enclose a formal response to the document you have served."

Doesn't that one line give their whole attitude away? One can almost guess the sort of thing that is coming next: "document you have served"? He's just written to say why he is unhappy – he hasn't "served" anything!

However this is what the "formal response" contained.

---

**William Albert Smith**

I make formal response to the Resolution Form served by the above-named on 6 February.

This case involved a Property Adjustment Order for Mr Smith and Mrs Green who had lived together and produced a child, and then a Contact Order in respect of the fruit of this unmarried coupling...The answer to his complaint lies with the procedures of the Court and is not in the hands of any solicitor. The Court diary is not listed to suit individual litigants...It is perfectly clear that we have no authority over Social Services...There was no undue delay on our part.

Mr Smith has seen fit to tick both boxes.

---

After the last sentence the writer might just as well have added "the complete idiot".

That is the perfect example of how it should not be done and commits just about every sin in the book in complaint handling.

It is arrogant, patronising, offensive, dismissive, sarcastic and belittling. They fail to identify the true cause of the problem, or if they do, they don't bother to explain it. They write using the third person. They use an adverb, which in effect is saying that it is obvious that solicitors have no control over social services and if you, Mr Smith, think any differently, you must be the world's biggest fool. Why on earth, in any event, should the client know that?

He whole thing is treated as if it was a claim being made against the firm, a slur on their professional ability and something that has to resisted at all costs. The whole attitude is 'here is a client who has had the gall to make a complaint. We must put him in his place and make him look ridiculous.'

Needless to say the whole thing escalated and got to the OSS. What a pity when, in all probability, all that was needed at that stage would have been to have talked to the client and the facts explained to him.

# PART THREE:
# CLIENT CARE

# CHAPTER ELEVEN
# CLIENT CARE:
# PRELIMINARY ISSUES

Before one can begin to take steps to achieve high standards of client care, it is necessary to gain an understanding of what client care really is and also to be convinced of the need to adopt a client care culture. It is fairly safe to say that, hitherto, this has assumed a low priority with solicitors' firms, one reason for this perhaps being the difficulty in measuring the success of such a culture in terms of profitability. Whatever the reason, unless one both understands what client care is all about and is convinced that it is right and necessary for your firm, any attempt at putting such a culture in place on a firm-wide basis is doomed to failure.

Unfortunately, there is no easy and universal definition of "client care", and, indeed, it may even mean different things to different firms.

In a Report to The Law Society, the Customer Management Consultancy Ltd said they took it to mean "the delivery of excellent customer service in a way that complements standards of professional conduct."

A large West Country firm spent ten months researching the concept and concluded "client care is a state of mind which should be woven into the daily workload as something that comes naturally, not put aside as a series of systems and processes to be filled in."

That could probably have been expressed a little more happily, but essentially they got the idea right. In some ways it may, firstly, be easier to define what Client Care is not.

It is apparent that many firms believe that because they, for instance, have a franchise or some other recognised system of work in place, it automatically means that their Client Care is up to scratch. Unfortunately, the two things do not necessarily follow and, indeed, it can be folly to think that they do. The reason is that it encourages a firm to believe that all they have to do is to follow the procedures that satisfy the Legal Services Commission, or whoever

controls qualifications for the system in question, and they are beyond criticism as far as their standards of service are concerned.

However, in reality, all they are doing is following a procedure that is, in effect,
a work system. Just because the system requires that the file be looked at, at
regular intervals so that it does not become overlooked, and even if it requires
a report to the client at regular intervals, it does not necessarily mean that the
client is being told what he wants to know, or, for example, why a decision was
taken not to pursue a particular line of enquiry that the client had suggested.

Indeed, too heavy a reliance on systems or procedures can be counter
productive simply because it fosters the conviction that if the procedure is
followed, then everything is being done correctly. It also encourages those
operating it to concentrate on compliance with the procedure to the exclusion
of other equally important considerations as far as Client Care is concerned.
Those considerations are much more to do with attitude of mind rather than
unthinking obedience to the demands of a procedure.

Procedures do, naturally, have their uses, but, in the context of Client Care,
their usefulness is limited and it is necessary to recognise procedures for what
they are and not to be misled into regarding them as the be-all-and-end-all.

Whilst on this issue, it may be worth reiterating that the CCS will not enquire
into complaints that, in effect, question the way in which a solicitor exercises
his, or her, professional judgement or how they choose to run a case. However,
they will expect that an explanation is given to the client, particularly if what is
done runs contrary to what the client had indicated he was expecting to be done.

It is particularly difficult for the general public to grasp the idea of what
service, where lawyers are concerned, is all about, which is, perhaps, not
surprising because this difficulty seems to be shared by a significant
percentage of lawyers themselves. The reason is that both confuse issues of
sub-standard work, that is to say issues of negligence, with issues of service.

If you go into a restaurant and the wine is corked, you know it is corked. Or if
you buy a pair of trousers and the seams come undone after a day's wear, you
know that what you have bought is not up to standard. It is not so easy with
lawyers, or for that matter with any professional. Even the best lawyers lose
cases.

There is a common misconception, as has already been referred to, that
because a job is done technically competently, the client has had good service
and has no grounds for complaint. This betrays a fundamental misunderstanding of what "service" is all about. It has nothing to do with technical
competence.

These days clients take for granted the fact that a solicitor knows how to do the job for which he is being paid. If he does not, it is not a complaint of inadequacy of service that he will be facing, but a negligence claim. In any event, the fact of the matter is that most clients will not know whether a job has been done badly, competently or excellently from a technical viewpoint. True, they may realise if a solicitor has made a complete hash of a job and will not be best pleased if a case is lost that they confidently expected to win. However, even in such cases, it is still possible for the client to be happy with the *service* that he received. What is more, if the client, in such circumstances, has received a good service, he is far more likely to blame his defeat on a biased judge or a lying opponent or some cause other than any shortcomings on the solicitor's part.

This misconception is starkly revealed in responses that the Consumer Complaints Service still gets to complaints about a solicitor's service which often are to the effect that "the client got what he wanted – it has not cost the client a penny" or "the job has now been completed and the client has got his money. Please confirm that is an end to this matter."

Such replies take no account of the fact that it may have taken, for example, three years to complete a job that should have taken no longer than three months and that, along the way, there are countless letters and telephone calls from the client that have been ignored.

So, having said what Client Care is not, let us examine in more detail what it is.

In a way, the whole of this book is relevant to the issues of Client Care, not just this section of it. Throughout, the reader will find advice which may be given in a specific context, but all of which is relevant to the question of how one goes about delivering a service that goes beyond what a client is expecting to receive. Good Client Care means doing that little bit extra so that a client's expectations are not just met – they are exceeded – and that must necessarily mean knowing what are the client's expectations in the first place, a matter dealt with in Part One, dealing with Complaints Avoidance.

The essential element involves having a firm-wide ethos and attitude of mind that means putting the client and his needs and convenience first and the needs and convenience of the office second. It also means that this ethos absolutely *must* permeate all the way through the firm, from the Senior Partner to the office junior and involves doing that little bit more that will result in the firm having a client who is happy and satisfied with the service for which he has paid. For a firm to have a client care policy that is going to succeed, it is essential that everyone in the firm knows what the policy of the firm is and actively participates in carrying it out.

If it is missing from any part of the firm, the whole strategy is doomed to failure. It only takes, for example, a disinterested telephonist, to destroy all the hard work put in by a conscientious partner who has worked diligently on a client's case.

Partners have a particular responsibility – they *must lead by example*. They cannot expect their staff to act and behave in a way that they are not seen to be doing themselves.

This does not mean, however, that every little whim of every client has to be accommodated. Indeed, if this were so, many solicitors would very soon find themselves up before the Disciplinary Tribunal, particularly where some of the more unusual requests from some criminal clients are concerned.

What sets solicitors in particular apart from others is that the profession is governed by Rules of Professional Conduct and Ethics. But even so, should a solicitor receive instructions with which he knows he would be wrong to comply, and therefore declines to do so, an explanation must still be given to the client so that he knows why the solicitor cannot do as he asks. He cannot just be ignored. If he is, particularly if things don't turn out the way the client wants them to, there is a ready-made complaint that the solicitor failed to follow instructions, albeit that the complaint should really be one of a failure to keep the client informed.

Similarly, the right messages must be transmitted from the top. If a firm has a senior partner who deals with all the wealthy and profitable commercial clients and who patently thinks that publicly funded work is a waste of time and that publicly funded clients are the dregs, that is fatal to the concept of client care. That attitude will transmit itself to junior staff and will then be reflected in their own approach to such clients.

In such circumstances there are a limited number of options available to the rest of the partners. They are:

1. the senior partner is persuaded to change his views; or

2. the firm stops doing legal aid work altogether; or, most drastically;

3. the rest of the partners get rid of the senior partner.

For a firm to succeed in practising good client care it **must**, throughout its entire structure, adopt the philosophy that **all** clients are equally important to the firm and are equally deserving of the same standards of service.

It is a fact that some staff just regard themselves as doing a job for nothing more than the pay packet at the end of the month. But it may be worth while asking them if they want to work for an organisation which is respected and of which they can be proud to be part – or do they really want to work for a firm for which no-one has any respect.

If it exists, that attitude must be changed. It will not be done overnight and it will need constant cajoling and reminders.

It is doubtful if it will be done by "preaching" to the staff in Biblical fashion, but, that does not mean that the staff as a whole should not addressed, for example, in a staff meeting. Indeed, that may be the best way to get over to everyone concerned the approach that the firm wants. It is the manner of the address which matters.

Some will readily and enthusiastically adopt the ideas propounded, others will be negative. Perhaps the best way to approach the latter is by having quiet one-to-one discussions. Even so, care must be taken to distinguish between those who, outwardly, may appear to have an antipathy towards the ideas being promulgated but who, in reality, are doing just what is wanted of them, from those who really are hostile to the whole idea.

Genuine antagonism to the concept of client care is rare. Having explained to staff that the firm is operating in a competitive environment and that, at the end of the day, their jobs depend on the firm's success, and that, in turn, depends on having happy and satisfied clients, most will readily implement the firm's policy in that respect.

Far more common than genuine antagonism is what could be described as an uncaring, or unthinking, attitude, where things continue to be done in the same way for no better reason than the fact that they have always been done that way.

Let us now look at the simple things that can be done at little or no cost to promote the feeling in the client that he is in good hands and is being looked after by a firm that is both competent and which cares about him and his affairs.

## PRACTICAL ASPECTS

### LETTERS

Standard letters that the firm has used for years are a prime example of the unthinking attitude referred to above, where things go on being done in the same old way just because that is how they have been done for years past.

Have a critical look at them at regular intervals. They may need scrapping and substituting by letters that are more relevant to changing times or are more client-friendly. This is particularly something to look out for if you are one of those firms that have been used to obtaining introductions to clients through some organisation e.g. a Trade Union or an Insurance Company. Impersonal letters of the type

> "You are requested to attend for interview with our Mr Bloggs at 2.00pm on Friday 4 October. Kindly telephone to confirm.",

or,

> "Dear Sir, Your contract documentation for your purchase of the above property is now ready for signature. Please make an appointment to call at the office for that purpose."

are just no longer acceptable and will immediately create totally the wrong relationship between the client and the firm.

Whilst on the subject of letters, it would be appropriate to make special mention of another relevant matter. Far too many letters are sent out with incorrect spelling and terrible grammar, not to mention those that are wrongly addressed. This, in itself, gives clients the impression that the firm is slipshod and has no pride in its work and, even more importantly, can lead to all kinds of recriminations if a neighbour, or the new owner of a property, opens the letter either by mistake or to find out where it has come from.

The problem stems from two sources. The first is that many secretaries type exactly what is dictated, usually because they are told that is what they are expected to do. It is very easy for the result to be ungrammatical. When speaking, using ungrammatical English is taken for granted and, sometimes, is never even noticed. Not so when it is written down on paper. What this means is that when dictating letters, particularly if this is done hurriedly, it is very easy to use ungrammatical English. Dictating machines make it easy to dictate as one thinks – and that does not always make for the best English because no proper thought is given to how the words are going to appear on a typewritten page.

The second problem then compounds the first. It is the failure by the author to read what he is signing, assuming, perhaps because of the existence of spell-checks on modern word processors, that everything will be correct.

However, spell checks do not indicate words that are spelt correctly, but used wrongly and the consequences could be disastrous. What a world of difference there is between "You can now sign the deed I sent you yesterday" and "You can not sign the deed I sent you yesterday". There is only one letter's difference between the two but get it wrong and it is one more claim on the firm's professional indemnity insurance and another increase in premium!

All this does not even take into account the disinterested typist who types away while gazing abstractedly at the far more interesting things that are happening outside, which means virtually anything and typing all kinds of rubbish.

The answer is that every letter should be carefully read, no matter how busy one is, before it is sent out. One of the benefits of modern word processors is that amendments are quick and easy to make and full use should be made of that facility.

## OFFICE FACILITIES

This is a commonly neglected area where it is all too easy to make a bad impression on the client which it is so easy to avoid. Remember, the objective is to make the client feel welcome, reassured and appreciated – you want his business and are prepared to look after him in every way.

The first essential is to ensure that all "front line" staff are operating in a way that the client is going to appreciate. By this I mean telephonists and receptionists. They are the first people connected with the firm with which the client, or potential client, will have contact and it is essential that they create the right impression.

Also it is they who will be responsible, from a day to day point of view, with the implementation of most of what follows in this section.

Firstly, is the reception area reasonably comfortable, or is it replete with hard, uncomfortable, chairs and have an air of austerity about it? If the latter, change it.

What kind of reading material is available for waiting clients? Do you have a cross selection of daily papers and magazines of general interest, or do you just have a few tatty copies of years old Readers Digests and magazines that reflect the Senior Partner's particular hobby, like copies of Coin Collectors Monthly?

Do you have anything to keep children occupied? Or are they allowed to run riot round the reception area, annoying all the other clients, with your prime Commercial Client desperately trying to avoid having the sticky fingers of a four year-old urchin, who seems to be attracted to him like a magnet, wiped all over his immaculate pin-stripe suit?

Is it even possible, if you have a general practice, to have separate waiting rooms for what we can term "respectable" clients and the "disreputable"? To avoid giving offence, the rooms could, for instance, be designated by allocating each to the relevant fee-earners who do the relevant type of work. Remember that, just as your Company Director will feel distinctly uncomfortable sitting in a room whose only other occupants are adorned with so much metal about their face and clothing that they could keep an average junk yard in business for a month, the reverse is actually true as well. Your rough criminal client is going to feel equally uncomfortable and out of place sitting in a room full of men wearing Chester Barrie suits and reading *The Times*.

All these are small things, but very important in creating the right atmosphere in which the individual client feels comfortable. And it goes further:

- Is your waiting area sufficiently removed from the earshot of the reception and telephone? If not, can you make it so? The reason is the question of confidentiality. How many times have you been in, for example, a pub and have been intrigued to overhear a conversation between two people who are total strangers to you, but who are talking about someone you know? Beware – the same kind of thing can happen all too easily in your Reception area.

- Is the receptionist supplied, as a matter of course, each morning with a list of each fee earners' appointments for the day? It is quite impressive for clients, especially those new to the firm, to be greeted by name.

- If a client is going to have to wait for a few minutes for his appointment, is he offered a coffee?

- Is the client fetched, by the fee-earner, from reception, or is he left to find his own way through a maze of corridors and stairs aided only by gabbled and half-understood instructions?

- If the fee-earner is not immediately available for the scheduled appointment, is the client told why? And if it is known that the fee-earner might be indefinitely delayed (he could, for instance, be unexpectedly held up in court), is the client told immediately, an apology proffered and the client given the opportunity to make another appointment? He may be annoyed at the inconvenience, but he is going to be a lot more annoyed if he is kept waiting for half an hour in anticipation and *then* has to make another appointment because he cannot wait any longer.

All these are little things and would cost little, for the most part, to put right, but are so important in creating the right atmosphere in which the client feels comfortable and valued.

Good client care requires you to look at things from the client's point of view and to appreciate matters from their perspective.

It means creating an atmosphere in which the client is comfortable and where he feels that he is valued and not just a nuisance or someone from whom you can extract money.

That old cliché 'this job would be OK if it were not for the clients' should never be heard, preferably not even in jest. Bear in mind that if the firm has no clients, then both it, and the firm's income, cease to exist.

Remember that many people are actually nervous at the prospect of using a solicitor and feel intimidated at just having to walk into the office. If they feel the same way on their second visit, then the firm's client care policy needs a distinct overhaul. If they still feel that way at the end of the job, then not only is the firm's client care policy either non-existent or a dismal failure, but it is an absolute certainty that that is one client the firm won't ever see again.

Bear in mind at all times that a satisfied client is the most effective advert a firm can have, while a dissatisfied client is, equally, the most effective form of self-destruction for any firm.

It is a widely quoted statistic that one satisfied client will recommend the firm to 5 other people, while a dissatisfied one will tell 23 others. If you doubt it, just consider your own experience in such matters. If you employ a plumber who does a great job for you, how many people do you tell? Maybe the odd friend if they should ask, over a pint, if you know of a good plumber. On the other hand, if you get a cowboy plumber, you can't wait to get down to the pub so you can tell anyone within earshot what an awful job this chap's done and advise them not to touch him with a bargepole.

And it gets worse. Research would suggest that only 5% of dissatisfied clients express that dissatisfaction to someone in authority. Followed to its logical conclusion, what that means is that for every complaint a firm is told about, it is statistically likely that there are 19 other people with the same complaint, and, if each of them are going to tell 23 others, it means that, as a result of one complaint, 437 people are going to think your firm is rubbish!

Likewise, when interviewing a client, the fee-earner should ensure he is not interrupted, by a telephone call or anything else. If that happens, the message to the client is, 'I don't care who you are, this other client is more important.'

## CHECKLIST

- Service not to be confused with technical competence
- Client first – firm second
- Involve the whole firm
- Partners lead by example
- Letters  – standard forms
  – spelling
  – grammar
  – accuracy
  – check before signing

- Office facilities  – staff
  – reception area – amenities; privacy
  – greeting the client

- Recommendations & reputation
- No interruptions

# CHAPTER TWELVE

# IMPLEMENTING A CLIENT CARE POLICY

So, having convinced yourself that there just might be something in this Client Care idea, how do you go about getting it across to the whole firm?

This is, of course, the hardest part. How many people know that it makes complete and absolute sense to give up smoking and resolve to do so, but all to no avail?

## TELLING THE STAFF

The first essential is, of course, to let the staff – all the staff – know what is being done, what are your aims and what is expected of them in playing their part in the whole objective.

But do not just tell them – ask them as well. Ask them if *they* have any ideas about how the firm can improve efficiency, the firm's relationship with its clients and what could be done to make clients more satisfied. That does not just apply to that moment in time either. Staff should be encouraged to come forward with ideas at any time. Consider rewarding, in some way, those who come up with good ideas – and let the rest of the staff know both about the idea and that it has been rewarded in some tangible way.

Never underestimate what your own employees can tell you. That is a mistake made by too many people at the top of organisations who think they know best about everything and there's nothing they can be told about their own company and area of work. If there is something basically wrong, it is often the staff who can tell you what it is and what needs doing to correct the situation. Likewise, do not ridicule any suggestion you get that may be considered to be unworkable or even stupid. That is a certain way to dry up the supply.

When you have got the message across orally, put it in writing as well. The staff manual, if the firm has one, is the obvious place for this.

## OLD HABITS DIE HARD

To get people in a firm with ingrained habits to change their ways can be a mammoth task, and even if a degree of success is achieved, it is all too easy for the bad old habits to re-emerge after a time.

Remember, this has to be, almost inevitably, a gradual, but unremitting, process. Things are not going to be changed overnight. But the approach must be both constant and consistent. Checks are going to have to be made to ensure that the firm's policy is being pursued in a proper way.

## CHECK SYSTEMS

For instance, introduce a system of making regular random checks on a number of files belonging to each fee-earner (and that includes partners) with the purpose of assessing all aspects of the matter from the "service" viewpoint, especially whether the client has been kept informed on a regular basis of relevant developments in his case. If there has been a gap of some weeks since the last letter was sent to him, has he been told why there would be such a gap? If not, and the gap was unexpected, why has an explanatory letter not been sent? That is, in fact, one of the most common causes for complaint and is a subject which is dealt with elsewhere.

At the same time, and by the same means, efforts could be made to try to identify areas where communication skills are lacking and the relevant people could then be provided with additional training in this respect. **No-one should be exempt** from this – not even the Senior Partner.

It would be only natural if partners felt insulted to have it suggested to them that they could communicate better with their clients and that they needed training, but the fact of the matter is that many do, but remember that it does not have to take the form of courses that they attend.

Suppose, for instance, that you come across a letter from one of your partners that prompted an unexpectedly unfavourable response from the client. A fresh pair of eyes, looking at it in an impersonal way, may well be able to spot why. One takes it for granted that your partner would not intentionally want to upset a client, so what went wrong? Could there have been a happier choice of words? Was the phraseology too brusque, and, if so, is this a charac-teristic of the person concerned?

If so, then have a quiet word with him. Point out the response his letter provoked and why you think it provoked that response. If the attitude is right and everyone understands that this is not intended as personal recrimination, and feels comfortable with the motives behind it, the person concerned will try to avoid repeating the same sort of thing in the future, but, in any event, future random checks will probably reveal whether that is the case.

It is an unfortunate fact that phrasing a letter so that the recipient does not put an unintended interpretation upon it can be harder than one thinks. More is said on that subject in the part of this book dealing with handling complaints, but it is a fact of life that once a client has a complaint, he will be only too inclined to put every unfavourable interpretation that he can on what he is told.

There are many instances where a solicitor against whom a complaint is made, has immediately acknowledged the fault and made a compensatory offer by way of recompense, only to find that the client's reaction has been to accuse him of trying to cover something up and to fob him off!

## USE THE COMPLAINTS RECORD

The other thing that a firm can, and should do is to learn from complaints which are raised. Every firm should have a Central Complaints Record. Regular checks of that Record should be carried out to see if there are discernable trends. Have there been complaints which could have been avoided? If so, has the necessary action been taken?

## USE STAFF AS AN EARLY WARNING SYSTEM

Your support staff can also be used as an early warning system for potential complaints, but they will probably only do this if they are asked to do so. So, ask them, or, rather, tell them to tell you. Remember, nothing avoids a fully-fledged complaint as much as their early diagnosis and resolution while they are still in the embryo stage.

Often a client who has a minor grumble will not bother to tell the fee-earner, but will, instead, make comments to the secretary or telephonist. Comments such as "What! He's not there again. Is he ever in the office?" or, in response to an offer to pass on a message, "Well, you can tell him, but he never returns my calls. Still, I suppose there's a first time for everything." must both be familiar strains to many support staff. Be warned, they are the first drifts of smoke that could easily develop into an inferno if not doused immediately *and the fee-earner should want to know about them*!

When they get the message, they should also *do something about it*, even if it is just an apology in passing. It is very flattering and impressive to a client for him to know that you are alive to his concerns before he has even mentioned them to the fee-earner personally.

One further matter relative to complaints. If a service complaint is made against a member of staff, please do not start taking them to task so that a blame culture starts to develop. Similarly, do not feel that the staff member has to be supported at all costs. But if one has to admit that the complaint is warranted, explain why to the person concerned in unemotional terms. Obviously if one person is attracting an unacceptable number of complaints, then something has to be done about it, but if people get the idea that a complaint is going, for example, to affect their chances of promotion, or a wage-rise, that is one sure way to ensure that they will stop seeking help if they feel they need it and they will tend to try to keep the existence of an unhappy client to themselves – usually with disastrous consequences.

## CUSTOMER SATISFACTION SURVEYS

Also, it is sensible to carry out, on a regular basis, Customer Satisfaction Surveys. These should be sent out when the job is concluded, with the bill if this is preferred, (and a stamped-addressed envelope) and should seek the client's reaction to the service he has received. The questions should be framed so that, initially they only require a "yes" or "no" answer with regard to various aspects of the service, or at least a simple choice of various answers achieved by ticking boxes. Only invite further comment or elucidation in the event of a negative response.

Such forms can be sent out with, say, every bill that the firm sends out in every fourth month.

There is, of course, one inherent risk with surveys that should be borne in mind. Most firms obtain the greater part of their income from repeat work for individual clients. If a client is surveyed and is in any degree critical of the service he received, his expectations are raised that you will do better next time because he expects you to be acting upon the information he has given you! If you do not, and he is surveyed again, he is likely to be more critical the second time around.

Interestingly, a recent survey showed that only a quarter of the firms in the country ever bothered to ask *any* of their clients how satisfied they were with the service afforded them, but only one firm in twenty canvassed *all* their clients in the same way. Only one third of firms made any kind of client care training mandatory for their staff.

There is one question that commonly arises with regard to these kinds of survey and it's this. 'If, as a result of sending out the form, we get a negative response, do we have to treat that response as a formal complaint and deal with it in accordance with our internal complaints procedure?' The answer to that is a guarded "no" but one should be aware that, in taking that line, a client may effectively be prevented from pursuing a genuine complaint or you may at least be running the risk that the client later says that he raised a complaint which the firm then ignored. The other alternative is that the client may have been intending to write a letter of complaint, but then refrains from doing so believing that he has raised the complaint with the firm by returning the questionnaire.

To guard against this, there are several courses that could be taken. For instance, the firm could delay sending out the survey until some weeks after the bill has been delivered. Perhaps more preferable, however, would be to endorse the survey form with a sentence to say that matters referred to in answers given are regarded only as giving information to the firm, and will not be treated as complaints requiring to be dealt with unless the client specifically indicates that he wishes them to be so treated. Even better would be to write separately to anyone appearing, by their responses, to indicate a complaint asking if they wished it to be dealt with as such.

In practice it is probably better to send out the form with the final bill or statement. This avoids the problems involved with delay in sending out the form, these being that the client is less likely to return it, there is additional expense to the firm and it may just get forgotten, and that the whole matter goes a bit stale.

---

### CHECKLIST

- Involve the staff
- Get rid of old habits
- Use check systems
- Use the Central Complaints Record
- Staff as an "early warning system"
- Customer satisfaction surveys

# PART FOUR:
# PRACTICE RULE 15
# & OTHER ISSUES

# CHAPTER THIRTEEN
# THE PROVISIONS OF THE RULE

Several aspects of the provisions of the new Rule have already been mentioned whilst dealing with what has gone before, but, for the sake of completeness, the salient points are gathered together, and what follows does include certain items that have not previously been mentioned.

The Solicitors Practice (Costs Information and Client Care) Amendment Rule 1999 replaced, as from 3 September 1999, the old Practice Rule 15. It encompasses the "Solicitors Costs Information and Client Care Code 1999".

The text of the new Rule, together with suggested Terms of Business Letters and Client Care Letters were included in a pull-out Supplement to the 21 April 1999 Edition of the *Gazette* and the text of the new Rule alone was also published in the edition of 24 March 1999. In addition, they can be found on the Law Society Web Site under "www.clientcare.lawsociety.org.uk." However, in the writer's view the wording could now be significantly improved and they could be made more "user-friendly", but they still serve as a good starting point.

The new Rule tightens up the old Rule, makes some additional provisions and makes it clear that there can be conduct implications for non-compliance.

In essence, Practice Rule 15 has two requirements – the giving of essential information to the client and dealing with complaints. The first of those two is, of course, designed to reduce the risk of the second arising.

It covers three main topics: costs information; responsibility for the job in hand and complaints handling.

The essential information which a client should have is usually achieved by means of Client Care letters.

There is a misconception amongst the profession that these are compulsory and must of necessity be literary works approaching the length of '*War and Peace*'. However, it is possible to write a perfectly good Client Care letter containing all the information required by Practice Rule 15 that is no more than eight lines long.

## COSTS INFORMATION

One of the main differences between the old & new Rule is that from September 1999 onwards, costs information is required to be in writing and to be given, not just at the outset of the matter, but at all appropriate stages throughout it, which information should be given clearly and in a way that is appropriate to, and capable of being understood by, the particular client and should not be inaccurate or misleading.

Many solicitors seemed to think that all that was required under the old Rule was that they had to stipulate their hourly charge out rate and there were many variations on the theme. Some merely gave the net charging rate, ignoring mark-up, VAT or disbursements. Others gave various combinations of those items.

The new Rule imposes an obligation on a solicitor to give the client the best information possible about the likely overall costs of a matter and makes it clear that a solicitor is expected to differentiate between profit costs, VAT and disbursements and, if the client is likely to be unfamiliar with the term, explain what the expression "disbursements" means.

"Best Information" means either:

1.   agreeing a fixed fee

2.   giving a realistic estimate or

3.   giving a forecast within a possible range of costs

Information about hourly rates is singularly useless without knowing how long a job is likely to take and, accordingly, a solicitor is now required, where time is a factor in calculating fees, to explain that and to give an estimate of the time likely to be spent on the matter. Solicitors may as well just give a realistic estimate or a forecast within a possible range of costs, which, as observed, with the addition of agreeing a fixed fee, are other acceptable alternatives. If it is not considered possible to give a realistic forecast, the solicitor should explain why and give the best possible information about the next step in the proceedings (but still try to give an overall possible figure, using different scenarios if necessary).

A private paying client should be told he can set an upper limit on costs, which figure should not be exceeded without the client's authority.

Consideration must be given as to whether the client is entitled to Legal Aid or has insurance cover available to him, and it must be borne in mind that consideration must be given to all the various forms of insurance that are available on the present market.

If a quotation or estimate is not intended to be fixed, say so clearly.

It must not be forgotten to keep the client informed throughout the matter with regard to the level costs have reached, and do so at least every six months. This is best done by rendering interim bills, which also helps the cash-flow! The six month period should be regarded as an absolute maximum and for preference the intervals should be shorter and the information should be given at any stage where the client may have cause to rethink his strategy, or at least would want to know the costs implications of what has happened.

In short, the client should also be kept fully informed about the costs implications of any development in the case, both as regards the solicitors own costs entitlement and as regards any potential costs liability the client may have towards any other party.

The solicitor must not forget to discuss the costs-risk/benefit implications of a matter and be prepared to demonstrate that this has been done.

It must also be remembered that the same considerations now also apply to cases in which the client is publicly-funded and it would be sensible to keep the client informed in this way even if it is anticipated the Statutory Charge will not apply. The only exception to this that springs to mind is where the client has public funding in a criminal matter.

Objections have been raised to the proposition that one must keep a publicly-funded client advised about accumulating costs in the same way as a private client because of the possibility of provoking a shoal of letters or telephone calls querying why you are telling the client about costs when he is publicly-funded. The reason, of course, is because it becomes very relevant should the statutory charge eventually apply and, in any event, it is no bad thing that clients should know the extent to which they are being supported by public funds.

A footnote on the matter of costs information. Try to avoid using the expression "profit costs". This can give clients the idea that all that money is going into your pocket and helps to foster the "fat cat" image. It would perhaps be better to use some less emotive expression, like "fees", and, if you wish to do so, there is no reason why a client should not be told, in broad terms, what has to be paid out of fees received.

## THE FEE-EARNER INVOLVED

What, in this context, should be put in a Client Care letter in order to comply with Rule 15?

1.  The name and status of the fee-earner who will be handling the client's affairs, remembering that if you are describing an employee as a Legal Executive he does have to be qualified as such and must be a Fellow of the Institute.

2.  If applicable, the name of the partner who has overall supervision of the matter and the name of the person the client can contact in the event of any concerns he has about the service provided. *Note: it is not necessary to even mention the word "complaint".*

It may also be wise to give some basic further information, like the name of the secretary with whom messages can be left if the fee-earner is unavailable, the office hours and anything else which is considered to be important, for example the times of day when the client would find it more likely to be able to make contact.

The requirement about the name and status of the fee-earner and the name of the person with overall supervision was also, in fact, a requirement of the Rule in its old form, a factor which was emphasised by the judgment in the case of *Pearless de Rougemont* v *Pilbrow*, to which further, more detailed, reference will be made shortly.

There are two aspects which flow from the requirement with regard to disclosing the status of the fee-earner.

The first is – just what does the word "status" mean? Does it mean the fee-earner's qualifications i.e. is he a partner, a solicitor, a legal executive etc? Or does it refer, as one ingenious solicitor suggested, to the fee-earner's status within the office i.e. partner, assistant, associate or litigation manager etc? The latter, of course would not mean having to say that the fee-earner is totally unqualified, although he may be very experienced in his field. It can well be imagined that solicitors might not want to effectively say to a client that the person who is going to deal with their case is totally unqualified, although that person may be well capable of doing the job and has been doing it perfectly adequately for years.

There is no definitive answer, but it has been suggested to those responsible for framing the Rules that they ought to give some guidance, although the spirit of the Rule surely means that the requirement is that the client should know what qualifications, if any, are possessed by the person handling his affairs.

However, that leads on to the second point, which is all to do with the case of Mr Pilbrow, (*Pearless de Rougemont v Pilbrow* [1999] 3 All ER 355) with which most solicitors will, by now, surely be familiar, but just to recap, as there appears to be a degree of misunderstanding in the profession about just what this case decided. Mr Pilbrow walked into the offices of the firm of Pearless de Rougemont and asked to see a solicitor. Many laymen make the same request and they do not really mean they want to see only a qualified solicitor as opposed to anyone who can deal with their affairs. Indeed, many laymen probably just assume that everyone who works in a solicitor's office is qualified.

In this case Mr Pilbrow was introduced to a lady who was totally unqualified, but very experienced and she acted for Mr Pilbrow to the conclusion of his case and the firm then submitted their bill. It was only at that stage that Mr Pilbrow realised that the fee-earner was not a solicitor and refused to pay the bill on the grounds that he had asked for a solicitor and had thought that that was what he had got. The court upheld Mr Pilbrow's claim, even though he had no complaint about the standards of workmanship, the result of his case or anything else.

The solicitors were, in this case their own worst enemy because they compounded matters by having failed to send out a Client Care letter disclosing the status of the fee-earner. Had they done so, Mr Pilbrow would have known he was not dealing with a qualified solicitor and as a result, his claim would, presumably, have failed.

However, if the solicitors had adopted the interpretation of the Rule that "status" meant the fee-earner's status within the office, he would still have been none the wiser.

You are warned. There is, in fact, no need to panic about *Pilbrow*. The judge only reached the decision he did because it was accepted by everyone that Mr Pilbrow had actually asked to see a solicitor and that was what he genuinely wanted.

If a client comes into the office and just asks to see someone about a particular matter, it does not mean that before he sees anyone there has to be a discussion with him about whether he wants a solicitor or not and that, if that does not happen, he will escape all responsibility for payment of the bill.

## COMPLAINTS HANDLING

It is interesting to note that neither the present Rule, nor the new one, actually says that a client has to be told to whom he can complain. The word "complain" or "complaint" is not mentioned.

What the new Rule actually says is that a client must be "told whom to contact about any problem with the service provided."

Words such as "Our aim is to give you a service that meets, or exceeds, your expectations. If you feel, at any time, that our service is falling below that standard, we would like to know and you can address your concerns to our Client Care Partner, Mr X." is perfectly adequate.

Nor is it necessary to supply the client with a copy of the firm's complaints procedure, or even, at that stage, to tell the client that there is one. This is another of those matters that the profession seems to have some difficulty in grasping. Even when solicitors have been specifically advised that they do not need to send out their complaints procedure to a client until the client actually complains and then asks for a copy, some still send it with their Client Care letters and then loudly complain that they are being required to invite complaints.

There was a possible difficulty here that involved the Legal Services Commission in their franchise requirements, at least in some areas, where practitioners were told they had to set out their Complaints Procedure in full in the Client Care letter. This, of course, went far beyond the requirements of Rule 15 but the explanation appeared to be that the LSC interpreted that as meaning that the client only had to be told to whom he can complain – a totally separate requirement of Rule 15! The writer understands that that has now changed.

Of course, one of the requirements of the Rule is that every firm must now have in place a written Complaints Procedure. Firms must ensure, and be prepared to show, that the procedure is reasonable, that complaints are dealt with in accordance with that procedure and ensure that, when it is appropriate to do so, the client is told of the procedure and given a copy.

Written complaints procedures seem to be the source of another problem for the profession. Many firms have in place what they fondly imagine to be a Complaints Procedure. Unfortunately, upon examination, these prove to be little more than statements of intent and certainly do not fulfil the purpose that was intended when the Rule was framed. Solicitors must bear in mind that, if they are requested to do so, they must produce a copy of the Procedure to the client. The obvious purpose behind this is that the client will know three things:

- **who** is going to deal with his complaints;
- **what** they are going to do; and, most importantly,
- **when** they are going to do it.

How many firms have complaints procedures that will do that? Experience would suggest there are precious few. A well-used excuse, if issue is taken on the subject, is "well, I've got a franchise and the LSC are happy our procedures comply with Rule 15". What is in place may satisfy the LSC, but that doesn't mean the procedure will satisfy Rule 15, of which the CCS are the arbiters – not the LSC.

Others rely on outdated precedents, of which there appear to be two main sources. One appears in the loose-leaf book *Keeping Clients* and the other is taken from a Law Society publication from some years ago *"Client Care – a Guide for Solicitors"*. The introduction to that publication states that it is meant as an internal document, but it is also misleading, because it refers to the fact that not all complaints are about service and some will be about minor issues, like delay or failing to keep the client informed. Thus the authors of that precedent themselves fell into the trap of mistaking technical excellence for service. Delay and failing to keep the client informed are, of course, the main issues of service about which complaints are made!

Every firm, indeed every practising solicitor in a firm with less than ten partners, should have received, in July 2000, a copy of the booklet *Effective Complaints Handling*. The Appendix to that booklet contains three specimen complaints procedures for different size firms and are reproduced in the Appendix to this book. If you have not done so, I recommend that you look at them and, if your firm's procedure doesn't match up, that you replace it with something on the lines of the appropriate specimen. If a copy of the booklet cannot be found, a telephone call to the Practice Standards Unit of the Law Society at Redditch, will procure a further, free, copy.

Sole practitioners face a unique difficulty in that they are likely to be seen as judge in their own cause if they deal with their own complaints. They might like to consider coming to an arrangement whereby other sole practitioners in their same geographical area will act as each other's complaint handlers. If this is done, however, remember to obtain from the client written confirmation that he is happy to go along with that arrangement, having regard to any potential breach of confidence.

Likewise if the complaint is made about the complaints handling partner himself, consideration should be given to allowing another partner to deal with the complaint

## Miscellaneous requirements

Do not overlook that, although what is mentioned above are the most important aspects of the requirements of Rule 15, there are a few others. These are:

- to tell a client about any reasonably foreseeable payments he may have to make, whether to you or anyone else and when they are likely to be needed

- to consider with the client how and when the costs will be paid

- to discuss any relevant costs risk/benefit analysis i.e. is what the client is seeking to recover worth the risk in costs that he is taking. This is a particularly important aspect of costs information in litigation matters and one that is frequently overlooked. It is also something that must be constantly borne in mind during the lifetime of every case so that appropriate advice can be given if, at any time, it appears that the costs at risk may be liable to exceed the potential benefit to the litigant.

Remember also that when first writing to the client there should be confirmed:

- the issues in the client's case

- the client's instructions

- any agreed plan of action i.e. what is going to be done next.

It would also be a good idea to tell the client when he can expect to be contacted again.

## Miscellaneous concerns

One matter that seems to cause endless queries is when is it not appropriate to provide all the information required by the Code. Practitioners should remember, that the onus is on them to justify not doing so if there is a complaint that costs information has not been given. Examples of where that would be the case are where repeat work is being undertaken on a regular basis for the same client, where compliance with the Rule would be insensitive e.g. making a deathbed will, or where it would be impractical e.g. an emergency injunction application, although, in that last instance, the relevant information should be given as soon as is practical thereafter.

The other main concern is that having given an estimate or quoted a range of costs, the figures are then cast in stone and cannot be varied.

To avoid that circumstance it would be wise to make the basis of the information clear at the first interview and to confirm that basis thereafter in writing and to make sure that continuing information is given about the costs incurred.

Complaints of that nature are far more likely if an estimate is given and it is not revised, even when the solicitor must know that it is going to be exceeded.

Another concern that is connected with the situation just considered arises from the common practice of asking clients to sign and return a copy of the Client Care letter as an indication of their agreement and authority for the solicitor to proceed on the terms set out in the letter.

Apart from the fact that this is, in itself a two-edged sword (what happens if the signed copy is not returned and yet work is done for which payment from the client is then sought?), it gives rise to a further question, which is whether the signed and returned copy is sufficient to constitute a Non-Contentious Business Agreement (N-CBA).

The position of regarding N-CBA's is covered by s57 Solicitors Act 1974 as amended. Subsection (2) provides that the agreement may provide for the remuneration of the solicitor either by reference to a gross amount i.e. a quotation, or by reference to an hourly rate (in which case the client can still allege that the hours charged for were not actually worked or were excessive), or by stipulating a commission or a percentage (e.g. in probate matters, 2% of the gross estate), or by the payment of a salary or "otherwise" i.e. by any other method. The terms may, or may not, include disbursements.

Provided the agreement is signed by the paying party, as it must be in the case given above, subject to exceptions with reference to taxation, it can be sued on as can any other agreement.

If the client applies for taxation and the solicitor seeks to rely on the agreement, in effect, the court can do as it likes.

Bearing in mind that the CCS has no jurisdiction to enquire into the amount of, or justification for, a solicitor's bill, the question, as far as the CCS is concerned, is largely academic, but can be relevant to the issue of the attitude that would be taken on an application for a Remuneration Certificate.

Reverting to basics, The Solicitors' Remuneration Order 1994 s 9(c) states that a client cannot require a solicitor to apply for a Remuneration Order where an N-CBA is in existence. This is because the fees are charged by reference to the Agreement rather than the factors referred to in s 3 of the Order.

The question, then, is whether the copy Client Care letter is capable of being an N-CBA. In other words we are back at the position propounded above.

It appears that the Courts take the view that, for the most part, signed copy Client Care letters are not regarded as N-CBA's because, to be regarded as such, N-CBAs have to be precise and unambiguous. Most Client Care letters do not fulfil that test, usually because they reserve variable hourly rates or mark-ups, or, for some other reason, are not capable of allowing the client to calculate precisely what the fee will be.

The same considerations would therefore be taken as applying to applications for a Remuneration Certificate, so that, for the most part, the CCS would not regard itself as being unable to entertain such an application.

## Sanctions

The Rule also indicates how breaches of its provisions will be treated. However, these appear to be completely illogical and the suspicion must be that those responsible for drafting it confused two scenarios.

What the Rule says is that material breaches of the Code that are not serious or persistent *"will be"* treated as evidence of an inadequate professional service. Non-material breaches will not be so treated. So far so good. However, the Rule then goes on to say that serious or persistent breaches of a material nature are a breach of the Rule and *"may be"* evidence of IPS. That would appear to be totally illogical. Non-serious breaches are evidence of IPS while serious breaches may be evidence of IPS.

Moreover, nobody appears to have yet defined what is a material or non-material breach of the Code.

However, in practice, what it means is that if a solicitor ignores the provisions of the Rule and there are multiple complaints to that effect, he is likely to be facing disciplinary proceedings as a result.

The sanctions available to the CCS on a finding of Inadequate Professional Services are:

- to disallow the firm's profit costs in whole or in part
- a compensatory award up to £5000 for Decisions made on or after 31 March 2000
- an order to rectify an error at the solicitor's own expense
- to direct the solicitor to take at the solicitor's own expense such action as shall be deemed necessary in the interests of the client

The imposition of any one or more of those sanctions does not preclude the imposition of one or more of the others.

One must also bear in mind the possibility of a Costs Order being made to reflect the cost of the CCS investigation. These have been set at a maximum of £840 but are discretionary. If the CCS Adjudicator considers a firm has made a genuine effort to resolve a complaint, whether or not it is justified, the Costs Order will not be imposed. Partial Costs Orders can also be made. As at the end of 2003 full Costs Orders had been made in only 12–13% of the eligible cases.

# CHAPTER FOURTEEN
# WHAT IS A COMPLAINT?

No complaints system will work unless the staff, including partners, recognise what amounts to a complaint that needs referring to the complaints partner and not be afraid to do so. That is more easily said than done.

All too often Rule 15 partners do not get to know about a complaint which has been made to a fee-earner until matters have gone too far down the road to damnation to be capable of rescue, or even worse, until the complainant has gone to the CCS.

There is a curiosity here. The University of West of England research showed that, although almost every firm had sent out a Client Care letter at the outset of their instructions, only 14% of clients said they had received one, and 59% denied having received one. Fee-earners need, therefore, to be alive to the distinct possibility that the client does not, in fact, know to whom he should be addressing his complaints, even if he has been told.

Frequently the client complains to the person handling his case, and only if the fee-earner fails to resolve the issue, when the client is getting really disenchanted, *might* the Rule 15 partner get to hear about it.

It is only natural that any employee is going to be wary of admitting to their employer that someone is unhappy with the way they are doing their work. It is something that has to be overcome and is all part of the Culture Change that often needs to take place if a firm is to adopt a proper Client Care philosophy.

How this is achieved is a matter for the individual firm. Each fee-earner can be seen individually and given individual assurances, or it can be done when the firm are all gathered together. However it is done, one thing is paramount. If staff (and partners) are going to be persuaded to be open about this, you must **never**, whatever the circumstances, criticise or recriminate with them. Do that and the word will spread like wildfire and will effectively put a stop to anyone ever telling you again if there is a problem.

By all means advise, or point out what the person could have done to avoid the situation which has arisen, but ensure that you do so in a spirit of encouragement.

One test of a complaint that should be reported is "Is this something I would really prefer that no-one else knew about?" If the answer is "yes" – it most certainly is something that should be reported.

One thing is for sure. Complaints do not just suddenly materialise from thin air. There are usually warning signs. Both solicitors and back-up staff have to be alert and receptive to any grumble and to act on it immediately. If it is not, that is when the problem begins to rankle with the client and it will, unless prompt steps are taken to resolve it, eventually surface along with the use of words like "uncaring" and "arrogant".

Hopefully the complaints partner will, in fact, know about the matter long before that stage is reached

Some firms require their fee-earners to ask the client, if it looks as if they may be complaining, whether they want to make a formal complaint, and, if that is their intention, they are then asked to put the complaint in writing, and are told it will then be referred to the Client Care Partner. At that stage, they are given a copy of the Complaint Procedure.

For reasons already given elsewhere, avoid asking, if possible, for the complaint to be put in writing. That means the client is being required to make his complaint on your terms and this can easily lead to accusations that the firm is unapproachable or places barriers in the way of clients who want to voice concerns. It is far better, at that stage, to offer the client an interview with the Client Care partner.

Remember, any expression of dissatisfaction which requires a response is a complaint. If the client thinks it is a complaint, then it is a complaint, whatever you or anyone else may think.

# CHAPTER FIFTEEN
# THE PROBLEM CLIENT

All that has been said so far relates to complaints received from the normal client, but, there are others and this is probably as good a time as any to say a word or two about them. Problem clients can manifest themselves in many ways and all practitioners will be familiar with them, not matter in which guise they come.

There are those who are dictatorial and, who, although they say they want your advice, are, in reality, more concerned about telling you how you should do your job; there are those who, no matter what might be done to try and manage their expectations from the outset, will still retain totally unreal ideas about what can be done and how quickly; then there are those who are unreasonably demanding and those who have no relationship with reality. No doubt there are other classifications which will also spring to mind.

No matter what description is applied, they all have one thing in common – they are all more likely to complain, for one reason or another, than the average client. The big question is – what can one do about them from the complaints point of view?

Sometimes the type is easily recognisable and will make his disposition known to you within minutes of entering your office and before you have accepted him as a client. The potential client who sits down and tells you that you are the fourth solicitor he's seen and all the rest were useless is, in fact, announcing, "I am going to be a pain in the neck", and, if you accept him as a client, you do so with eyes wide shut! You must know, in your own mind, that you are running a real risk of having to cope with a difficult client and, into the bargain, one from whom you can expect problems that will more than likely take some considerable time to resolve at no little cost to yourself. We have not yet reached the situation where solicitors are forced to take on clients they would rather not act for, so, if you do not want to run the risk of trouble, the best advice is to invent an excuse and get rid of them.

Some, however, are more subtle, and it is only when you have been acting for them for some time that their true nature is revealed. Those who are professional complainers are usually skilled at doing this and inventing grounds of complaint that would never occur to the ordinary client.

It is essential, when you know you have a problem client, that you are extra careful to ensure that, when the inevitable complaint comes, you are ready for it and can, in all honesty, maintain that the client has no grounds on which the complaint can be justified.

Herein lies a problem, however. Because of the nature of the complainant, there is a great temptation, when the inevitable complaint is made, to dismiss it out of hand, on the basis that the complaint is only being made *because* the client is difficult. That is precisely the wrong thing to do. Just to dismiss a complaint in that way is inviting further problems where the normal client is concerned. That is even more the case with the problem client, who has often convinced himself that you are not fit to be in practice and who is just looking for further fuel to stoke the fire of his discontent.

There is also a temptation to classify a client as difficult or unreasonable *because* they complain or to believe that all complaints are made by such people. That simply is not the case. In fact, only a relatively small proportion of complaints that reach the CCS are from such clients or those that are motivated by considerations other than a genuine belief that they have had a raw deal.

With the problem client you may correctly suspect that whatever you say, reasonable and true though it may be, is not going to be accepted, but that is no reason not to answer the complaint properly, and the CCS will certainly expect you to do so. If you do not deal with the complaint at face value, you may, when the client then refers his complaint to the CCS, find yourself penalised for failing to deal with the complaint properly under Rule 15 – even if the complaint itself is found to be unsubstantiated!

You may think that to be unfair, but you will be missing the point, which is that you have not even properly considered whether there might, in fact, be some justification for the complaint. You have dismissed the complaint on the supposition that because the client is difficult his complaint cannot be justified. The two things do not follow.

It is essential that, even when complaints are made by unreasonable people, or are themselves unreasonable, they are still dealt with properly in accordance with your firm's complaints procedure.

You may have to accept that, no matter what you do, you are not going to satisfy this type of complainant and, no matter what, they are going to refer the matter to the CCS. Nonetheless, if proper steps are taken to try to resolve the matter direct with the client, and a proper letter of explanation is eventually written, it is going to save a lot of time and trouble when the CCS does eventually ask you for your response to the complaint and to explain how you have tried to deal with it.

There is one situation that seems to particularly exercise practitioners. That is where the solicitor wishes to acquaint the CCS with factors that they do not wish to be disclosed to the complainant. It is assumed, rightly, that the CCS operates on a basis of open disclosure of all communications made to it and if, for instance, they say in a letter that the complainant is mentally unstable, and that is disclosed to him, not only will it only inflame matters, but could also, in some cases, have dangerous consequences for the firm and its personnel.

The answer in such cases is to write two letters to the CCS, one which can be disclosed, and another clearly marked that it is not to be disclosed, which sets out what you want to say about the complainant on a personal basis insofar as you believe it has relevance to the complaints made.

However, a word of caution. If the relevant complaint is the subject of a formal decision of an Adjudicator of the CCS or goes to appeal, nothing will be placed before the Adjudicator or the Appeal Committee that has not been disclosed to both sides.

Finally, under this heading, something ought to be said about the abusive complainant. There are, unfortunately, certain people who find it necessary, not just to be rude, but to be abusive and/or threatening and, sometimes, obscene. Such behaviour can be distressing and worrying, especially when female members of staff are made the recipients.

No-one expects you to have to meekly accept this kind of behaviour, but, do remember that in such cases you may have to justify your decision not to have anything further to do with such people who, it must be remembered, usually deny vehemently the behaviour alleged against them.

If the abuse is made over the telephone, the steps that should be taken are to make a note of what is being said – and it should be verbatim as far as is possible, no matter how embarrassing it may be for the person concerned. The person taking the call should calmly and politely say that should the caller continue in the same vein, the call will be discontinued. Should the abuse carry on, the receiver can then be replaced, and, if appropriate, the Rule 15 partner informed and the note placed on the relevant file.

Should such calls be persistent, the caller can be informed verbally that no more calls will be accepted from him and a letter written to that effect confirming that staff have instructions not to accept the client's calls.

If the abuse is written, all that is simply required is a letter asking the writer to stop writing in such terms and explaining that, even with the best will in the world, it makes it impossible to have a meaningful and constructive dialogue if such emotive language is used.

Perhaps the worst scenario is when such behaviour takes place in the office. Again a note should be made of what happens and what is said. If a female member of staff is the subject of the abuse, she should call for assistance from a male member of staff if she requires it. The client should be politely asked to leave the premises and, if he refuses, there is very little alternative but to call the police.

Finally a word about the persistent complainer. There are those who come back time and again with the same complaints, sometimes wrapping them up in a different package, but with essentially the same content. You are not expected to have to deal with the same thing time after time.

Often the opportunity for these complaints is provided because the solicitor has not addressed the complaint properly in the first place and has not agreed with the client what his complaints are or amount to. If that has been done and the agreed matters have been dealt with, you can then either send a letter pointing out that the complaints are merely repeats of those that have already been dealt with, even if dressed up differently, and that there is nothing more that you wish to say, or it can be pointed out that you have dealt with what the client agreed represented all his complaints and it is not now open to him to move the goal-posts. If the complainant still persists, send a polite letter to the effect that you will not be responding to any further letters on the subject – there is a limit to the duty to reply to a client's correspondence!

# APPENDIX

## IMPORTANT NOTE

The time scales used in these precedents are not mandatory and can be altered to suit the individual firm.

The precedents set out various alternatives. If any one of them is not applicable or available to any firm, the inappropriate choice should be omitted.

## MODEL COMPLAINTS PROCEDURE
(for use by sole practitioners)

### *The Procedure*

Although not essential, in making your complaint it would be helpful to me if you could provide details of your concerns in writing (if you have not already done so). If you would prefer not to have to do this, please arrange to see me and I will be pleased to take details from you.

### *What will happen next?*

**Timescale**

1.  I will acknowledge receipt of your complaint, set out my understanding of it and request your confirmation or seek any necessary clarification. I will also confirm who will deal with your complaint should this not be myself.  
*Within 2 days of its receipt*

2.  I will register your complaint in my Central Register (for monitoring and management information purposes) and open separate a file.  
*Within 1 day of receipt of complaint*

3.  I will acknowledge receipt of your confirmation letter or telephone call and confirm what will happen next.  
*Within 1 day*

4.  I will then commence investigating your complaint. This may involve one or more of the following steps:

    (a)  if I acted for you personally I will consider your complaint in the light of what the file reveals and the details of your complaint. I will then write to you with my detailed response or invite you to a meeting to discuss the matter.  
*Within 10 days*

    **OR**

    (b)  I will ask the person who acted for you to provide me with a response to your complaint within 5 days.  
*Within 1 day*

    (c)  I will then examine the response and the file as against your complaint and, if necessary, speak to the person who acted for you.  
*Within 3 days of receipt of the response and file*

    **OR**

    (d)  as an alternative to a), b) and c) above, I will ask another independent local solicitor to investigate your complaint using the steps set out at a) above and then to report his findings to me.  
*Within 3 days*

**Timescale**

5. I will then write to you inviting you to meet with me
   to discuss and hopefully resolve your complaint.

   *Within a
   further 3 days*

6. If a meeting is declined or is for some reason impractical
   I will write to you with a detailed response to your
   complaint and with any suggestions I have for resolving
   it to our mutual satisfaction.

   *Within 5 days
   of completing
   the
   investigation*

7. If a meeting between us takes place I will still write to
   you to confirm what took place and detailing any
   agreed solution that was arrived at.

   *Within 2 days
   of the meeting*

8. If, at a meeting or from your written reply to my
   detailed written response, you remain dissatisfied with
   what I have said and how I propose resolving your
   complaint, I will arrange for my decision to be reviewed.
   This may happen in one of the following ways:

   (a) my own review of my handling of your complaint
       and why you are dissatisfied with my decision,

   *Within 5 days*

   OR

   (b) By arranging for someone else in the firm who is
       entirely unconnected with the complaint to review
       how it was handled and the decision taken.

   *Within
   10 days*

   OR

   (c) by asking my Local Law Society or another local
       firm of solicitors to review my handling of, and the
       decision on, your complaint (if they are willing to
       do this).

   *Within
   10 days*

   OR

   (d) by inviting you to agree to a process of formal
       mediation through an independent mediator
       (if this is available).

   *Within 5 days*

   Note: the timescale for concluding the review
         process at c) and d) above will need to be
         agreed with the individuals involved but you
         will be told how long the process will take.

9. After the review has taken place you will be informed of
   the outcome. This will review my initial handling of
   your complaint and my decision on it.

   *Within 5 days
   of the
   conclusion
   of the review*

10. If you still remain dissatisfied with how your complaint     *Within 5 days*
    has been handled and the decision on it, I will write to
    you confirming my final position on your complaint
    and explaining why I consider my handling of, and
    decision on, it (and of any review) was reasonable. I will
    also supply you with the name and address of The Office
    for the Supervision of Solicitors, the solicitors' regulatory
    body to whom you may refer your complaint once I
    have concluded my professional obligation to try and
    resolve it.

    **Please note:** changes to any of the above timescales
    will be confirmed to you together with
    an explanation.

## MODEL COMPLAINTS PROCEDURE
(for use by small firms)

### The Procedure

Although not essential, in making your complaint it would be helpful to us if you could provide details of your concerns in writing (if you have not already done so). However, should you prefer not to do this, please could you arrange to see our Client care partner, Mr....................., who will be pleased to take details from you.

### What will happen next?

|  |  | Timescale |
|---|---|---|
| 1. | We will acknowledge receipt of your complaint, set out our understanding of it and request your confirmation or seek any necessary clarification. We will also confirm who will deal with your complaint. | *Within 2 days of its receipt* |
| 2. | We will register your complaint in our Central Register (for monitoring and management information purposes) and open a separate file. | *Within 1 day of receipt of complaint* |
| 3. | We will acknowledge receipt of your confirmation letter or telephone call and confirm what will happen next. | *Within 1 day* |
| 4. | We will then commence investigating your complaint. This will normally involve the following steps: |  |
| (a) | The complaint will be referred to Mr              , our Client Care partner. | *Within 3 days* |
| (b) | he will ask the person who acted for you to provide him with a response to your complaint within 5 days. | *Within 3 days* |
| (c) | he will then examine the response and the file as against your complaint and, if necessary, speak to the person who acted for you. | *Within 3 days of receipt of the response and file* |
| 5. | Mr              will then write to you inviting you to meet with him to discuss and hopefully resolve your complaint. | *Within a further 3 days* |
| 6. | If a meeting is declined or is for some reason impractical Mr              will write to you with a detailed response to your complaint and with any suggestions he has for resolving it to our mutual satisfaction. | *Within 5 days of completing the investigation* |

**Timescale**

7. If a meeting between us takes place Mr       will still write to you to confirm what took place and detailing any agreed solution that was arrived at. — *Within 2 days of the meeting*

8. If, at a meeting or from your written reply to Mr      's detailed written response, you remain dissatisfied with what he says and how it is proposed to resolve your complaint we will arrange for the decision to be reviewed. This may happen in one of the following ways:

    (a) another partner of the firm may review of Mr      's handling of your complaint and why you are dissatisfied with the decision, — *Within 10 days*

    **OR**

    (b) we may ask our Local Law Society or another local firm of solicitors to review our handling of and the decision on your complaint (if they are willing to do this). — *Within 5 days*

    (c) we may invite you to agree to a process of formal mediation through an independent mediator (if this is available). — *Within 5 days*

    **Note:** the timescale for concluding the review process at (b) and (c) above will need to be agreed with the individuals involved but you will be told how long the process will take.

9. After the review has taken place you will be informed of the outcome. This will review our initial handling of your complaint and our decision on it. — *Within 5 days of the conclusion of the review*

10. If you still remain dissatisfied with how your complaint has been handled and the decision on it, we will write to you confirming our final position on your complaint and explaining why we consider our handling of, and decision on, it (and of any review) was reasonable. We will also supply you with the name and address of The Office for the Supervision of Solicitors, the solicitors' regulatory body to whom you may refer your complaint once we have concluded our professional obligation to try and resolve it. — *Within 5 days*

    **Please note:** changes to any of the above timescales will be confirmed to you with an explanation of why.

## MODEL COMPLAINTS PROCEDURE
(for use by multi-office or larger firms)

*The Procedure*

Although not essential, in making your complaint it would be helpful to us if you could provide details of your concerns in writing (if you have not already done so). If you prefer not to do this, please could you arrange to see either of the persons mentioned below, who will be pleased to take details from you. If in writing, your complaint should be addressed to the Firm's Client Care Partner, who is.........................
and who works from the firm's office
at...............................................................

While *Mr.................. will retain overall responsibility for the handling of your complaint, the steps set out below will be undertaken by Mr.................., the partner in charge of the Department/Branch Office concerned to whom he will send the details of your complaint and who will accept the initial responsibility for dealing with the complaint.

*What will happen next?*

| | | Timescale |
|---|---|---|
| 1. | We will acknowledge receipt of your complaint, set out our understanding of it and request your confirmation or seek any necessary clarification. We will also confirm, at that stage, who will be dealing with your complaint. | *Within 2 days of its receipt* |
| 2. | The complaint will be registered in Central Register (for monitoring and management information purposes) and a separate file opened. | *Within 1 day of receipt of complaint* |
| 3. | We will acknowledge receipt of your confirmation letter or telephone call and confirm what will happen next. | *Within 3 days* |
| 4. | We will then commence investigating your complaint. This may involve one or more of the following steps: | |
| | (a) the person who acted for you will be asked to provide a response to your complaint within 5 days. | *Within 3 days* |
| | (b) the response will then be examined together with the file and your complaint and, if necessary, further information will be sought from the person who acted for you. | *Within 3 days of receipt of the response and file* |
| 5. | You will then be invited to meet Mr.................. to discuss, and hopefully resolve, your complaint. | *Within a further 3 days* |

|  |  | **Timescale** |
|---|---|---|
| 6. | If a meeting is declined or is for some reason impractical We will write to you with a detailed response to your complaint and with any suggestions we have for resolving it to our mutual satisfaction. | *Within 5 days of completing the investigation* |
| 7. | If a meeting between us takes place we will still write to you to confirm what took place and any agreed solution that was arrived at. | *Within 2 days of the meeting* |

8.  If, at a meeting or from your written reply to our
    detailed written response, you remain dissatisfied with
    what we said and how we proposed resolving your
    complaint we will arrange for our decision to be
    reviewed. This may happen in one of the following ways:

|  |  |  |
|---|---|---|
| (a) | Mr................ may review his own handling of your complaint and why you are dissatisfied with his decision, | *Within 5 days* |

    **OR**

|  |  |  |
|---|---|---|
| (b) | by arranging for someone else or a small number of people in the firm who are entirely unconnected with the complaint to review the complaint, the response, the file and any other relevant information, how the complaint was handled and the decision on it. | *Within 10 days* *Within 10 days* |

    **OR**

|  |  |  |
|---|---|---|
| (c) | Mr................., our Client Care partner may review the complaint by taking the steps set out at (b) above | *Within 10 days* |

(d)  by asking our Local Law Society or another local
     firm of solicitors to review our handling of, and the
     decision on, your complaint (if they are willing to
     do this).

(e)  by inviting you to agree to a process of formal
     mediation through an independent mediator (if this
     is available).

> **Note:** the timescale for concluding the review
> process at d) and e) above will need to be
> agreed with the individuals involved but you
> will be told how long the process will take.

|  | **Timescale** |
|--|--|

9. After the review has taken place you will be informed of the outcome. This will review our initial handling of your complaint and our decision on it.

*Within 5 days of the conclusion of the review*

10. If you still remain dissatisfied with how your complaint has been handled and the decision on it, we will write to you confirming our final position on your complaint and explaining why we consider our handling of, and decision on, it (and of any review) was reasonable. We will also supply you with the name and address of The Office for the Supervision of Solicitors, the solicitors' regulatory body to whom you may refer your complaint once we have concluded our professional obligation to try and resolve it.

*Within 5 days*

**Please note:** changes to any of the above timescales will be confirmed to you with an explanation of why.

## CENTRAL COMPLAINT REGISTER

The centrally maintained complaints register should include, possibly in column format, the following:

- Reference number of complaint
- Date of complaint
- Name of client
- Identity of fee-earner
- General nature of complaint(s)
- Date file examined
- Date of meeting (if any)
- Which complaints justified
- Reasons complaint made
- Details of any offer or other proposal & date
- Date of any review
- Date final letter sent
- Date file closed
- Action to be taken internally as a result of complaint

# INTERNAL COMPLAINTS PROCESS

Fee-earners, and staff generally, will be aware that this firm has in place a Complaints Procedure that sets out the steps that will be followed by the Rule 15 partner in dealing with any complaints that are brought to his notice. While it is useful for everyone to be aware of the procedures that will be followed, the Procedure itself is mainly for the benefit of the client.

As far as members of staff (which includes everyone, both fee-earners and non-fee-earners) are concerned, it is considered that it would be helpful to go further and to give additional guidance on issues of concern.

The first of these is **what counts as a complaint** that should be reported to the Rule 15 partner?

The short, but unhelpful, answer is – anything that the client thinks is a complaint. That, however, begs the question of how you know what the client might be thinking.

The answer is – if in doubt, ask the client. It is always open to anyone to whom concerns are being addressed, to ask the client if they are making a formal complaint that they would like to be dealt with under the firm's Complaints Procedure.

However, the following should be referred to the Rule 15 partner automatically:

- Anything that could be construed as a complaint which is expressed in writing (but clients should not be required to put their complaints in writing)

- Any concern that the client specifically says is a complaint

- Anything raised by a client about your own handling of a matter that you would rather no-one else knew about

Very often it is a matter of degree. For example, a comment that one telephone call was not returned when the client was told it would be, would not be of sufficient gravity to necessitate being reported. A comment that telephone calls were never returned would be.

Non-fee-earners, particularly secretaries, telephone and reception staff, should report to the fee-earner concerned any comment that they receive that hints at a potential problem in the making. For example, if, on offering to pass on a message to a fee-earner to call the client back, a comment is made such as "If he does, it will be the first time" or anything similar, should be reported to the fee-earner, who should then, even if only in passing, offer an apology to the client.

The over-riding consideration, at all times, must be to resolve clients' concerns as quickly as possible. This can not only preserve the clients' goodwill, but also can save the firm considerable expense in lost fee-earning time that would be expended in dealing with a fully-blown complaint that reached the CCS.

Staff are assured that complaints that are notified to the Rule 15 partner will not reflect unfavourably on the fee-earner concerned. It is recognised that no-one is perfect and everyone will occasionally make mistakes. Furthermore, complaints can result from a variety of causes which will not always be within the control of the fee-earner concerned e.g. a clash of personality, pressure of work etc.

Only in the most serious cases will disciplinary action be considered. Preventative measures such as training where necessary, or even the amendment of the firm's procedures will always be a first consideration if any specific action on the part of the firm is considered necessary.

It should also be understood that complaints can actually assist the firm in improving its relations with clients as they let us know where the client thinks we are failing and where our procedures and practices could be improved. It is therefore vital that the firm has this information, which it won't have unless complaints are passed on, so that a central record can be kept for analysis purposes.

# INDEX

# Publishing for Management

*Management*

| | | |
|---|---|---|
| **Business Management for Solicitors** | David Porter<br>2002  £38 | Ideal companion for a new partner or practice manager. |

*Litigation*

| | | |
|---|---|---|
| **Fixed Costs** | Kerry Underwood<br>2004  £32 | Making fixed costs work in practice. |

*Accounts*

| | | |
|---|---|---|
| **Credit Management for Law Firms** | Julia Walden<br>1999  £38 | Practice and procedure for better cash collection |

*Marketing*

| | | |
|---|---|---|
| **Solicitor's Manual of Marketing** | Ian Cooper<br>2001  £275 | Looseleaf collection of precedents, with commentary on advertising and marketing materials |
| **How to Get the Fees You Deserve** | Ian Cooper<br>2001  £49 | Marketing to maximise fees |
| **Marketing to Existing Clients** | Ian Cooper<br>2001  £49 | Materials and ideas to maximise cross-selling |

*Skills Audio Tapes*

| | | |
|---|---|---|
| **Effective Time Management** | Tony Hackett<br>1999  £45+VAT | Making the most of time for fee-earners and staff alike. |
| **Effective Telephone Skills** | Tony Hackett<br>1995  £36+VAT | For staff training on telephone skills. |
| **Effective Presentation Skills** | Avril Carson<br>1996  £42 + VAT | Aimed at solicitors who wish to develop their professionalism in presentations. |

*(Prices correct at time of printing – check on our website before ordering.)*

## xpl publishing

31–33 Stonehills House, Howardsgate, Welwyn Garden City,
Hertfordshire, AL8 6PU
Tel: 01707 334823    Fax: 01707 335022
E-mail: sales@xplpublishing.com    Website: www.xplpublishing.com

Printed in the United Kingdom
by Lightning Source UK Ltd.
102307UKS00001B/91-94

9 781858 113289